Isidore Fishman, M.A., Ph.D.

REMEMBER
THE DAYS OF OLD

An Introduction to Biblical History

VALLENTINE, MITCHELL - LONDON

First published in Great Britain 1969
by Vallentine, Mitchell & Co. Ltd.
18, Cursitor Street
London E.C.4.

SBN: 85303033 2

Printed and bound in Great Britain by
The Garden City Press Limited
Letchworth, Hertfordshire

To My DEAR DAUGHTER
HELEN ON HER
BIRTHDAY DECEMBER 28th
1971.

REMEMBER THE DAYS OF OLD

For Fiona

REMEMBER THE DAYS OF OLD

Remember the days of old,
Consider the years of many generations;
Ask thy father, and he will declare unto thee,
Thine elders, and they will tell thee.

DEUTERONOMY, CHAPTER 32, VERSE 7

CONTENTS

ILLUSTRATIONS

PREFACE

THE purpose of this book is to provide the pupil with an insight into Biblical history. The Bible is not simply a record of human endeavour, of heroic episodes and of dramatic events. It is primarily a book which deals with the relationship of man to God, and of man to his neighbour. Mankind, it teaches, can reach the greatest heights only by responding to the Divine call to lead a responsible life. Moreover, the Bible has a special significance for the Jewish people, chosen by God to carry out the mission of spreading His message of 'righteousness and justice' among mankind. As the story unfolds itself, we shall find that the facts speak for themselves. Obedience to God's laws brings peace and satisfaction. Disobedience, on the other hand, especially in the days of the Judges and of the two Kingdoms, ends in disaster. The successful efforts of Ezra and Nehemiah to bring the people nearer to God by establishing the inspired teachings of the Torah as the supreme authority provide the Jewish people with a fresh impetus. The written word, supplemented by oral tradition, was to prove the main source of Israel's miraculous preservation through the ages.

An introduction to Biblical history obviously cannot deal exhaustively with such a vast subject. I have limited my approach to a portrayal of major events, adhering closely to the Biblical narrative. The student should constantly refer to the sources, and familiarize himself with their contents. Suggestions for readings from the Bible, together with exercises based on the subject-matter, are made at the end of each chapter.

The difficulty of assigning dates to early events is well known, but we are on safer ground when we reach the period of the monarchy, from the ninth century B.C.E. The discovery of contemporaneous monuments and inscriptions enables us to determine, with some precision, the year when an important event took place. Some of these confirm or shed light on the Biblical narrative, and are referred to in the course of this book. Archaeologists and specialists are still at work, and it is quite possible that the name of the Pharaoh of Egypt or the exact date of the fall of Jericho will one day become known. I have relied, in the main, on the findings of modern scholars, though they themselves are often at variance.

I wish to express my gratitude to Mr. T. Shahar who read my manuscript, and made a number of valuable suggestions, which have been incorporated in this work.

The illustrations and maps are reproduced by kind permission of the Youth and Education Department of the Jewish National Fund.

ISIDORE FISHMAN

1

ABRAHAM

In the beginning

WHEN God created the universe, He blessed man with the power to reason for himself and to tell the difference between right and wrong. Unfortunately, mankind proved unworthy of these blessings. After the death of Adam and Eve, wickedness increased, and frequent acts of violence were committed by man against his neighbour. Men defied God's purpose, which was to have a world based on the principles of justice, righteousness and peace. Had it not been for the righteous Noah, the entire human race would have been swept away by the great flood. By God's command, Noah and his immediate family took shelter in the ark, and were saved. The earth became peopled again through the descendants of Noah's sons, Shem, Ham, and Japheth, who founded many nations.

The Sumerians occupy Mesopotamia

The tenth chapter of the Book of Genesis tells us about the races and peoples who were scattered over the earth after the unsuccessful attempt to build the tower of Babel, in the plain of Shinar. This fertile region later became known as Mesopotamia, because it lay 'between the rivers' Tigris and Euphrates, and was much sought after by nomadic tribes. A clear picture of their history has been given us by scholars, who have managed to read the many inscriptions on clay tablets which have been excavated in the area. About the year 2800 B.C.E., they tell us, a very intelligent tribe, called the Sumerians, occupied Mesopotamia for five hundred years. They were then driven out by a race called the Akkadians who, after a

1

century, were themselves overthrown. Eventually, a certain Ur-Nammu, described as 'King of Sumer and Akkad', founded the Third Dynasty of Ur which lasted from about 2060 to 1950 B.C.E.

Ur of the Chaldees

We begin our story of the Jewish people in the twentieth century before the Common Era, and focus our attention on the city of Ur, then a thriving sea-port at the head of the Persian Gulf. Ur was one of the chief cities founded by the Sumerians, and the discoveries made by archaeologists on the site where it once stood are truly astonishing. These prove beyond doubt that the Sumerians enjoyed a high level of civilization and material comfort. They were, for example, pioneers in the art of writing, lived comfortably in well-built brick houses and many were engaged in commerce and agriculture. Gold and silver ornaments of exquisite beauty, made by skilled craftsmen, have been discovered in the royal tombs. Led by their priests, the people in every city worshipped numerous gods on the tops of ziggurats (big mounds shaped liked pyramids). The most important deity at Ur was the moon-goddess, Sin, to whom human sacrifices were offered, and its ziggurat, which has been unearthed, had a base two hundred feet long and one hundred and fifty feet wide, with a tower seventy feet high.

One of the citizens of Ur at this time was Terah, the father of Abram, Nahor, and Haran.

Abram declares his belief in God

In the middle of the twentieth century B.C.E., Ur was invaded from the east by a people called the Elamites. This may well be the reason why Terah decided to leave with his family for the land of Canaan. But when he arrived at Haran, in the north of Mesopotamia, he decided to settle there. Abram had long realized how degrading it was to believe in gods of wood and stone. His heart and mind convinced him that there must be one supreme and invisible Power, the Creator of heaven and earth, who guided the daily lives and actions of men with justice and righteousness. Because of his outstanding faith and conviction, Abram was singled out by God to become the father of the Jewish nation.

2

*Abram obeys the
Divine command and
journeys to Canaan*

Abram was seventy-five years old when he received the Divine call to leave his native country, where they worshipped idols, and to proceed to another land where he would become the founder of a people devoted to the service of the one and only God. Through his teachings and example, he was told, all the families of the earth would be blessed. Without hesitation, he obeyed the summons and left Haran, journeying southwards towards the land of Canaan, accompanied by Sarai, his wife, Lot, his nephew, and the members of his household. They drove their flocks and herds before them, pitching their tents wherever they halted. Abram eventually arrived at Canaan in the vale of Shechem, where he learned, in a new revelation, that the land he had entered was the very one his descendants would inherit. Canaan was inhabited by numerous tribes, who, like the peoples of Ur and Haran, also worshipped idols. However, Abram was not afraid to announce that he believed in God when he built an altar near Bethel, the next stage of his journey. In his new surroundings, Abram and his family became known as Hebrews, i.e., people coming from 'the other side' of the river Euphrates.

After a short stay in Egypt, owing to a famine in Canaan, Abram and Lot returned to the neighbourhood of Bethel. By this time they possessed large flocks, and quarrels broke out between their herdsmen as there was insufficient pastureland and water to supply all their needs. To avoid conflict, Abram suggested that he and Lot separate, and generously offered his nephew the first choice of land in which to settle. Lot chose the fruitful valley of the Jordan and lived in the town of Sodom, notorious for the wickedness of its inhabitants. Abram, after being reassured by God that his descendants would inherit Canaan, settled in the oak-groves of Mamre, in the plain of Hebron.

The peaceful life of Abram was suddenly disturbed by a war which threatened the safety of his nephew Lot. Five rulers of small cities in the south, among them Sodom and Gomorrah, revolted against their conqueror Chedorlaomer, the powerful king of Elam, to whom they had paid tribute for twelve years. Chedorlaomer, with the aid of three neighbouring kings, declared war on them, and, sweeping down from the north, overcame all opposition. He put an end to the revolt by defeating the rebels in the vale of Siddim by the Salt Sea. The victors sacked the cities of Sodom and Gomorrah and began their return northwards, taking with them numerous captives, among them Lot. On hearing of his nephew's plight, Abram, aided by three friendly Amorite princes, led three hundred and eighteen of his trained men against the invaders and overtook them at Dan, in the extreme north. Dividing his men into groups, Abram launched a surprise attack at night, and the enemy fled in disorder.

The pursuit continued as far as Hobah, north of Damascus, all the booty was recovered, and Lot and his fellow-captives were rescued. On his way home Abram met Melchizedek, the king and priest of Jerusalem, who praised God for defeating the enemy. Melchizedek blessed the patriarch and was given a tenth of all the spoils as a thanksgiving offering. Abram returned the rest of the booty to the king of Sodom, but refused to accept any part of it as a reward for his services. His only request was that a share should go to those who had helped him in battle.

Abram is assured that Sarai will bear him an heir

Abram still had no son, and it seemed that his heir would be his chief steward, Eliezer of Damascus. This made him unhappy, but God revealed Himself to him and comforted him. In a vision, God made a promise that Abram would have a son and countless descendants. Though they would eventually live in a strange land and serve their masters for four hundred years, they would return with a great deal of wealth and occupy Canaan from the river of Egypt to the Euphrates.

As Sarai remained childless, she gave her Egyptian maidservant, Hagar, to Abram as a second wife. Soon, Hagar was expecting a child, and became insolent towards her mistress. Sarai, after complaining to Abram, treated her maidservant so harshly that Hagar fled into the wilderness. An angel appeared to Hagar and told her to return home, promising that she would give birth to a son, whom she was to call Ishmael. Hagar returned to Mamre where her child was born.

Thirteen years passed by, and in the patriarch's ninety-ninth year God again appeared to him and made a solemn covenant that Abram would become the ancestor of many nations and that Canaan would belong to his descendants. He was also told that Sarai would bear him a son, to be named Isaac, through whom the promise would be fulfilled. Abram would now be called Abraham, 'father of a multitude' (of nations), and Sarai would be renamed Sarah, 'princess'. In obedience to this sacred covenant, Abraham was commanded to circumcise himself and all the males of his household; in future every male child was to be circumcised when he was eight days old.

The wicked cities of Sodom and Gomorrah are destroyed

Of all the people in Canaan, those living in the cities of Sodom and Gomorrah were the most wicked. They committed acts of violence, and had little regard for the life or property of others. One day, as Abraham sat at the entrance of his tent, he saw three men approaching and, with his usual courtesy, invited them in for a meal. These men were in fact God's messengers and they announced that Sarah's son would be born a year later. When his visitors left, Abraham accompanied them part of the way, and was then told of God's intention to destroy the cities of Sodom and Gomorrah. The patriarch heard the news with dismay, and pleading that the righteous should not be destroyed, obtained God's promise to pardon the guilty cities if at least ten righteous men could be found. Two of the messengers arrived at Sodom and accepted Lot's invitation to stay in his house, but the men of the city were so sinful that they tried to harm them and were therefore struck with blindness. It was obvious that there was not a single righteous man to be found. Urged on by the Divine messengers, Lot and his family escaped and made for the nearby city of Zoar; Sodom and Gomorrah were utterly destroyed by a sudden downpour of fire and brimstone (sulphur). Lot's wife looked back and, caught by the lava, turned into 'a pillar of salt'.

Isaac is born, and Ishmael is sent away

Abraham was living in Beersheba when Sarah gave birth to a son, who was named Isaac. Ishmael still regarded himself as his father's heir, and some two or three years later, made fun of a celebration held on the day when Isaac was weaned. Sarah noticed his rude behaviour, and urged Abraham to send Hagar and her son away. Although grieved, Abraham agreed to her request, for God had told him that Ishmael, too, would be the ancestor of a mighty nation. Hagar and her son wandered about in the wilderness of Beersheba and were almost dying of thirst when she suddenly saw a well of water. God told her of her son's great future, and she made her home in the desert. Ishmael grew up, became an archer, and lived in the wilderness of Paran where he married an Egyptian woman.

Abraham faces his greatest trial

Throughout his long life, Abraham had shown complete faith in God. Now that he had an heir, he hoped to end his days in peace but the greatest test was yet to come. Abraham was told by God to sacrifice Isaac as a burnt offering on one of

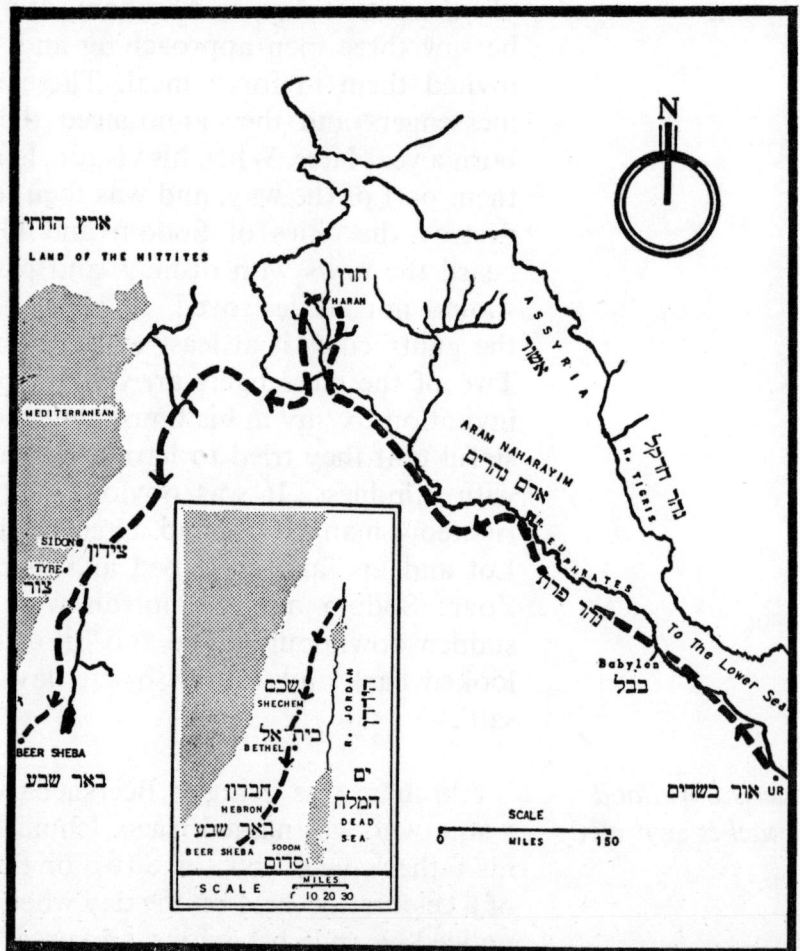

Abraham's Journeys

the mountains in the land of Moriah. Though bewildered by this command, the patriarch did not falter. He rose early in the morning, saddled his ass, and, with two servants in attendance, brought his son to the appointed place. Isaac submitted without a murmur to being bound on the altar, but when Abraham took hold of the knife, the Divine voice told him not to lay his hand on the lad, since all that God desired was proof of his willingness to obey. A ram, entangled by its horns in a thicket, was offered up instead and God, praising Abraham, promised that his seed would be numerous.

Abraham purchases the cave of Machpelah as a family grave

Abraham again made his home at Mamre, happy in the knowledge that his son Isaac would succeed him. Before long, he lost his lifelong companion Sarah, who died at the age of one hundred and twenty-seven. Courteously refusing the offer of the Hittites who owned the territory to use their sepulchres or accept one of them as a gift, Abraham bought the nearby cave of Machpelah as a burying-place from Ephron, the Hittite, for the sum of four hundred shekels' weight of silver. The field and cave of Machpelah thus became a family possession.

מערת המכפלה

Cave of Machpelah; Hebron

Eliezer, at his master's request, finds a wife for Isaac

Abraham was naturally concerned about Isaac's future. He did not want his son to marry a Canaanite woman, who might turn him away from God. So Abraham sent his servant Eliezer to the city of Haran in Mesopotamia, where his brother Nahor still lived, to find a suitable wife from among the members of his own family. Outside the city, the servant rested for a while near a well, and earnestly prayed that the girl who came to draw water and offered him and his camels drink would be Isaac's future wife. This turned out to be Rebekah, the granddaughter of Nahor, Abraham's brother. Eliezer was welcomed at the house of Bethuel and Laban, Rebekah's father and brother, to whom he told the purpose of his mission. Bethuel, realizing that it was God's will, consented to the request for Rebekah's hand in marriage to Isaac. After a few days, Rebekah set out for Canaan, met Isaac and married him.

Abraham's death

Abraham married another wife, Keturah, through whom he became the ancestor of many Arab tribes. To ensure peace among the members of his family, Abraham gave Isaac his property, and after presenting his other sons with gifts, sent them away to make their homes in the land of Arabia. He died at the age of one hundred and seventy-five and was buried by his sons, Isaac and Ishmael, in the family grave at Machpelah.

Readings from the Bible

Genesis, chapter 12, verses 1 to 9	Call of Abram
Genesis, chapter 18, verses 20 to 33	Abraham's plea for Sodom
Genesis, chapter 22, verses 1 to 19	Abraham's greatest trial
Genesis, chapter 24	Eliezer finds a wife for Isaac

Exercises

1. Draw a map and trace Abraham's journeys from Ur to Shechem.
2. 'Abraham was a man of deep faith, generosity and humility.' Illustrate this statement by incidents in the patriarch's life.
3. Write briefly on the following:
   (*a*) Ur of the Chaldees; (*b*) Lot; (*c*) Eliezer of Damascus; (*d*) Ishmael; (*e*) The cave of Machpelah.
4. How far does archaeology help us to understand the Bible?

2

ISAAC AND JACOB

Esau sells his birthright

ISAAC was the worthy son of an illustrious father. In his youth, he had already shown his complete trust in God, and after Abraham's death was blessed with Divine guidance. Both he and Rebekah lived happily together but were disappointed that they had no children, although they had been married for twenty years. Isaac prayed earnestly to God, and Rebekah became the mother of twin sons, entirely different in nature and character. Esau, the elder, was born, as the Bible tells us, with a reddish complexion and hairy skin, and became a skilful hunter, whilst Jacob, the younger, led a peaceful life as a shepherd. Each parent had a favourite son — Isaac loved Esau, while Rebekah preferred Jacob. On one occasion, when he came back hungry and tired from hunting, Esau agreed to sell his birthright to Jacob in return for some bread and lentil pottage. Esau obviously had little regard for the privilege of being first-born and succeeding his father as head of the family. Nor did he care for his parents' feelings, and displeased them by marrying two women who belonged to the pagan tribe of the Hittites.

Isaac stays for a time in Gerar

Isaac made his home in the neighbourhood of Beersheba, and owned pasture-land, flocks and herds. He remained on peaceful terms with the Canaanites, and we know of only one incident which caused him some anxiety. Owing to a famine, he went to live among the Philistines in the city of Gerar. He worked very hard, acquired rich crops and many cattle, and became the envy of his neighbours. Abimelech, king of Gerar, was anxious to avoid any quarrels, so he requested Isaac to depart. The peace-loving Isaac immediately left and encamped in the nearby valley, only to face more trouble when his herdsmen had a dispute with the herdsmen of Gerar over the ownership of certain wells. Isaac finally settled in Beersheba itself and, before long, received a visit from Abimelech, who, recognizing that Isaac was favoured by God, concluded a peace treaty with him.

Isaac blesses Jacob, mistaking him for Esau

Isaac had grown old and blind, and obviously did not realize that Esau, by his conduct, was unworthy of his trust. Feeling that his end was near, Isaac decided to confirm Esau's authority as first-born. He told his son to bring him his favourite dish of venison, and he would bless him. Rebekah, overhearing the conversation, dressed Jacob in his brother's clothes, covered his hands and neck in goat-skin, and sent him in to Isaac with some savoury meat she had prepared. Isaac's suspicions were aroused when he heard Jacob's voice asking for the blessing, but when he felt his hands he believed that Esau was with him. He blessed Jacob and told him that his descendants would inherit a fertile land and rule over other nations.

No sooner had Jacob left than Esau returned and the truth was discovered, but Isaac did not withdraw the former blessing. In response to Esau's plea, he foretold that the future generations of Esau would live by the sword and would have to serve Jacob's descendants for some time. In a rage, Esau vowed to kill his brother as soon as their father died, so Rebekah advised her favourite son to leave home and stay with Laban, her brother, at Haran. She secured Isaac's consent by suggesting that Jacob should seek a suitable wife, and not follow his brother's example by marrying a Hittite woman.

After Jacob had left Beersheba, Esau, in an effort to make up to his parents for having married foreign wives, married his cousin, a daughter of Ishmael.

Jacob has a remarkable dream

On his journey from Beersheba towards Haran, Jacob came to the city of Luz and rested for the night in the open air. There he dreamed that angels were ascending and descending a ladder stretching from earth towards heaven. God appeared to him and promised that the land would belong to his descendants and that he would return home under His protection. To mark the spot where he had the vision, Jacob set up the stone on which he had slept, and renamed the place Bethel, which means 'the House of God'. He vowed that if he returned safely to his father's house he would regard this as a sacred place and would offer God a tenth of all he owned.

Laban makes use of Jacob for his own ends

When Jacob reached the outskirts of Haran, some shepherds told him that Rachel, Laban's daughter, was coming to the well to draw water for her father's sheep. When she arrived, Jacob rolled away the stone covering the well, drew water for her flock, and then introduced himself to Rachel, who quickly ran to inform her father that he was there. Jacob was welcomed by Laban and, falling in love with Rachel, undertook to work as his shepherd for seven years in return for her hand in marriage. Laban agreed, but when the time had expired, he brought his elder daughter Leah to the marriage ceremony instead of Rachel. As the bride was heavily veiled, Jacob discovered the deception only after she had become his wife. When he asked Laban why he had deceived him, Laban offered the excuse that it was the custom for the elder daughter to be married first. Jacob had no choice but to accept the situation, and married Rachel also, after which he served another seven years for her. Leah and Rachel, and their maidservants Zilpah and Bilhah, bore him eleven sons and one daughter. Of these, Reuben, Simeon, Levi, Judah, Issachar, Zebulun and a daughter Dinah, were born to Leah; Dan and Naphtali to Bilhah; Gad and Asher to Zilpah; and Joseph to Rachel.

At the end of the fourteen years Jacob wished to return home, but Laban persuaded him to stay by promising him all the speckled and spotted sheep and goats among the flock he tended. The crafty Laban, true to his nature, removed all the marked sheep from his flock, sending them away with his sons to a distant place. Through a clever plan, Jacob got the better of Laban, so that the unmarked sheep bore speckled and spotted lambs which he could then claim as his own.

Jacob leaves for home

Another six years passed by and Jacob prospered, but he could no longer endure the envy and jealousy of Laban and his sons. So he decided to return to his father's home in Canaan and, while his father-in-law was away shearing his sheep, he left Haran with his wives, children and cattle. Three days later Laban was told of Jacob's departure and pursued him, overtaking him in the highlands of Gilead. Laban's anger was increased by the loss of his *teraphim*, i.e., house gods, which Rachel had secretly taken away with her without Jacob's knowledge. Laban had been warned by God not to threaten Jacob in any way. When he met his son-in-law, he reproached him for leaving so suddenly, and accused him of theft. Jacob strongly denied this and reminded Laban how hard he had worked for him during the past twenty years. Eventually Laban's anger subsided, and they parted on friendly terms.

The two brothers meet

Jacob was approaching the land of Edom where his brother, Esau, had settled. Fearful for the safety of his family, Jacob sent a message of goodwill to his brother but was told that Esau was approaching with four hundred men. Preparing for the worst, Jacob divided his camp into two parts, so that if one were attacked the other might escape. He prayed to God for deliverance, and sent a succession of valuable gifts to Esau to pacify him.

That night Jacob sent his wives and children across the ford of Jabbok, and stayed behind alone. A 'man' appeared and wrestled with him until dawn. The man, who was an angel of God, could not defeat Jacob, so he touched the hollow of his thigh and lamed him. Nevertheless, Jacob refused to release his opponent from his grasp unless he received a blessing. His wish was granted, and the angel told him that from now on he was to be called by a new name, Israel, which means 'he who strives with God'. To commemorate this unique experience, Jacob called the name of the place Peniel, because he had seen 'God face to face', yet his life had been spared.

When Jacob met Esau, his brother embraced him affectionately, which was surprising. Sensibly refusing the offer of an armed escort, Jacob parted from Esau in peace, and eventually arrived at Shechem.

Isaac is buried in the cave of Machpelah

Jacob stayed at Shechem for some time and then continued his journey home. He halted at Bethel, where he had once stayed the night, and erected an altar in thanks to God for his deliverance from danger. As Jacob reached Bethlehem he suffered a tragic loss, for his beloved wife Rachel died whilst giving birth to her younger son, Benjamin. Rachel was buried in the heights of Bethlehem and Jacob set up a memorial stone over her grave. After thirty years' absence from home, Jacob reached Hebron, where Isaac was now living, and was there reunited with his father. Isaac died at the age of one hundred and eighty, and his sons Esau and Jacob were present at his burial in the cave of Machpelah.

Rachel's Tomb, Bethlehem

Readings from the Bible

Genesis, chapter 25, verses 27 to 34	Esau sells his birthright
Genesis, chapter 27	Isaac's blessing
Genesis, chapter 28, verses 10 to 22	Jacob's dream
Genesis, chapter 32, verses 23 to 33	Jacob wrestles with an angel

Exercises

1. Draw a map and insert the places which Jacob visited during his wanderings.
2. Explain why Esau was unworthy of being his father's heir.
3. In our prayers, we often come across the phrase, 'the god of Abraham, Isaac and Jacob'. Why did the patriarchs deserve this great honour?
4. What incidents occurred at the following places?
   (*a*) Gerar; (*b*) Bethel; (*c*) the river Jabbok; (*d*) Bethlehem; (*e*) Hebron.

3

JOSEPH

*Joseph's dreams
arouse his brothers'
envy*

JACOB had settled down comfortably in Hebron and, for miles around, his sons looked after his numerous flocks and herds. Joseph, who was now seventeen years old, was his special favourite. Rather thoughtlessly, his father presented him with a gift of a 'coat of many colours', which was a long-sleeved garment, worn, in those days, by men of high rank. This in itself was enough to make his brothers envious, but they became even more resentful when Joseph told them of his two dreams. In the first, their sheaves bowed down to his sheaf standing upright in their midst. In the second, the sun, moon and stars bowed down to him. These dreams seemed to mean that one day Joseph would rule over all the members of his family.

*Joseph is sold
into slavery*

While the brothers were taking care of Jacob's flocks in the pasture of Dothan, a place near Shechem, Jacob sent Joseph to see how they were. Seeing him in the distance, they plotted to kill him, throw his body into a pit and then say that he had been eaten by a wild beast. Reuben, the eldest, persuaded them not to shed any blood, but to throw Joseph into the pit alive, hoping to save him after the others had left. When Joseph arrived they stripped off his coat and threw him into the pit.

Suddenly, they saw a caravan of Midianites and Ishmaelites carrying spices from Gilead to Egypt, and, on Judah's advice, they sold Joseph to the merchants for twenty pieces of silver. This made Reuben, who was away at the time, very sad indeed. The brothers then dipped the coat in the blood of a he-goat

14

and brought it to their father, who, thinking that Joseph had been devoured by a wild beast, mourned his son for many days. Meanwhile, the caravan arrived in Egypt and Joseph was sold as a slave to Potiphar, a captain of the Guard.

During the seventeenth century B.C.E., when these events possibly took place, Egypt was ruled by the Hyksos, a word meaning 'foreign rulers', who had come as conquerors from Syria. Their dynasty lasted for about one hundred and sixty years.

Joseph interprets the dreams of Pharaoh's butler and baker

Joseph performed his duties so successfully that he was soon appointed overseer of his master's entire household. Unfortunately, Potiphar's wife falsely accused him of insulting her and Joseph was thrown into prison. Through his ability and industry, he soon gained the governor's confidence and was placed in charge of the other prisoners. Two royal officers, the chief butler and the chief baker, who had offended the king, were also in custody awaiting their trial and both had a dream which they asked Joseph to interpret. The butler's dream, in which he pressed grapes growing on a three-branched vine into Pharaoh's cup meant, said Joseph, that he would be restored to his office in three days. The baker's dream of birds pecking bread from the uppermost of three baskets he carried on his head meant that he would be hanged in three days. Joseph requested the butler to plead for him before Pharaoh and secure his release from prison. Three days later, on the king's birthday, the baker was executed and the butler was pardoned, but forgot Joseph.

Pharaoh is troubled by two extraordinary dreams

Two years passed and Pharaoh had two dreams. In the first, seven lean cows ate seven well-fed cows, and in the second, seven thin ears of corn swallowed up seven full ears of corn. Troubled by his dreams which, he felt, must have an important meaning, Pharaoh could find no interpreter. It was then that the chief butler remembered Joseph and told Pharaoh what had happened in prison.

Hastily summoned before Pharaoh, Joseph explained that the king's dreams meant that seven years of great plenty would be followed by seven years of severe famine. He advised the appointment of an intelligent and wise person, with authority to take possession of one-fifth of the land. It would be his responsibility to store corn during the seven years of plenty to prepare for the seven years of famine. Pharaoh could find no better choice than Joseph himself who, at the age of thirty, became the chief governor of Egypt. Joseph stored corn in granaries throughout the land, and when the famine came the stocks were released and sold to the Egyptians.

Meanwhile Joseph had married Asenath, the daughter of Potiphera, the priest of On, who bore him two sons. He gave them Hebrew names, calling the first-born Manasseh, and the second, Ephraim.

The brothers go to Egypt to buy corn

The famine was not confined to Egypt but extended to the neighbouring country of Canaan. Jacob urged his sons to go down to Egypt to buy corn but he kept Benjamin back, in case he came to harm. On their arrival, they presented themselves before the governor. Although twenty-two years had passed since he had last seen them, Joseph recognized his brothers immediately. They, however, had no idea that the royal governor had once shared their home in Hebron. Joseph wished to be quite sure they were truly repentant of the crime they had committed against him, so, through an interpreter, Joseph spoke harshly and accused them of being spies. This they strongly denied. They were twelve brothers, they said; the youngest had been left at home with his father, and another had disappeared. If this were true, answered Joseph, one of them should fetch the young brother while the others were imprisoned, and he placed them all in custody.

After three days, they were released and Joseph allowed them to take corn back home for their families, but they were to return to Egypt with Benjamin so that their story could be checked. Simeon alone was to be retained as a hostage. The brothers looked at each other in fear, and their consciences began to worry them. Speaking to each other in the Hebrew language, they admitted how guilty they felt for treating Joseph so brutally, and were reminded by Reuben how he had tried to save him. Joseph, who understood the conversation, turned aside and wept.

On the way, one of them opened his sack to give his ass food and found the money he had paid for the corn, not knowing

16

that this had been restored at Joseph's command. On reaching home, they told Jacob all about their experiences, and were terrified to find, when emptying their sacks, that each had had his money returned. Jacob still refused to let Benjamin go to Egypt in case he would be exposed to danger.

The brothers pay a second visit to Egypt

The famine in Canaan became so severe that Jacob had no alternative but to yield to Judah, who offered to be personally responsible for Benjamin's safety. The brothers took with them double the money necessary to pay for the corn, and gifts of the choicest fruits. Accompanied by Benjamin, they again appeared before Joseph, who, through his steward, invited them to dine with him. This only added to their fears, and they approached the steward and explained how they had found the money in their sacks when returning to Canaan. He replied that the money must have been a gift from God as the price of the corn had been paid. Simeon was released from custody, and when Joseph arrived for the meal he was presented with Jacob's gifts, but, on seeing Benjamin, he retired to his private room and wept with emotion. After a while, he rejoined his brothers, who were astonished to find they were placed at the table in order of their age.

When they had left, Joseph ordered his men to supply them with corn, to return their money secretly and to place his silver divining goblet in Benjamin's sack. The brothers set out early next morning, but were soon overtaken by the steward who accused them of theft and ingratitude. When the goblet was discovered in Benjamin's sack, they tore their clothes in grief and returned to the city. Judah offered to become Joseph's slave in place of Benjamin, but Joseph refused to detain anyone but the offender. Benjamin, he said, would be held and the rest were free to return to their father.

Joseph reveals his identity

Judah then approached Joseph and made a moving and eloquent appeal. He begged that Benjamin be returned to his aged father who had already lost one son and would die of grief if yet another were taken from him. Joseph could no longer restrain himself and, ordering everyone except the brothers to leave, told them who he really was. The brothers were speechless with fright, but Joseph told them not to reproach themselves for selling him to Egypt as it had been God's will that the people should not die of starvation. He urged them to return to Canaan and hurry back with their father, their families, and flocks and herds. They would live in the land of Goshen, the finest pasture-land in Egypt, and have sufficient food for the remaining five years of famine. When the news reached Pharaoh he, too, invited them to settle in Egypt and ordered that wagons be sent to convey Jacob and his household. Joseph presented them with gifts and they returned to Canaan.

Jacob meets his long-lost son

When Jacob was told that Joseph was still alive, he could hardly believe the news, but, after hearing the full story, set out on his journey, accompanied by sixty-six of his direct descendants and their families. He stopped on his way at Beersheba where God appeared in a vision and told him not to be afraid of going to Egypt, for his descendants would return to Canaan. On their arrival in Egypt, Jacob was presented to Pharaoh, and blessed him.

The famine had reached a critical stage and all the money of the Egyptians and Canaanites had passed into the royal treasury. In exchange for food, the Egyptians were now required to hand over their cattle and then to sell their lands to Pharaoh. They were still to be allowed to cultivate their soil, provided they paid a tax equal to one-fifth of what they produced, but the land belonging to the priests was exempt.

The Israelites settled happily in the land of Goshen and became prosperous.

Jacob blesses Joseph and his sons

Jacob had reached the ripe old age of one hundred and forty-seven. As the end of his life was approaching, he sent for Joseph and made him swear that he would not bury him in Egypt but in the land of Canaan, in the resting place of his fathers. Jacob became very ill and Joseph went to visit him with his two sons, Manasseh and Ephraim. The dying patriarch blessed them and then called all his other sons to his bedside. In prophetic words, he summed up their personal qualities and foretold their future destinies. After repeating his wish to be buried in the cave of Machpelah, Jacob died. Joseph ordered that the body be embalmed, and mourning was observed for

18

seventy days. Then, with Pharaoh's permission, Joseph and all his brothers, together with the elders of Israel and Egypt and a military retinue, carried Jacob's body into Canaan and he was buried in the cave of Machpelah.

Joseph's dying wish to be buried in Canaan

On their return to Egypt, Joseph's brothers, afraid that Joseph would seek revenge, asked his pardon for their past deeds, but Joseph assured them that he no longer bore any grudge against them. Joseph survived his father by fifty-four years and before he died, at the age of one hundred and ten, made the Israelites take an oath to carry his remains with them when God brought them back to the Promised Land (see pages 24 and 48). Joseph's body was embalmed and placed in a sarcophagus.

Readings from the Bible

Genesis, chapter 37, verses 1 to 11	Joseph's dreams
Genesis, chapters 40 and 41	Pharaoh appoints Joseph as governor of Egypt
Genesis, chapter 44, verses 18 to 34	Judah's plea

Exercises

1. Find the land of Goshen on the map. Why was it considered the most fertile part of Egypt?
2. Describe, in your own words, Joseph's and Pharaoh's dreams. What was their interpretation?
3. Can you suggest why Joseph waited so long before he informed Jacob that he was still alive?
4. Try and find out more about the Hyksos, who were the rulers of Egypt. (Your local library will have books on the subject.)

4

MOSES

Pharaoh enslaves
the Israelites

ABOUT the year 1550 B.C.E., the Hyksos (see page 15) were finally expelled from Egypt after a successful uprising led by Ahmose, a prince of Thebes, an ancient city on the river Nile. Ahmose and his successors looked upon the Israelites with suspicion, because of their friendly relations with the former rulers, and took measures to deprive them of their freedom. Their final degradation occurred during the reign of a king who, the Bible tells us, 'knew not Joseph'. Scholars have not been able to agree about who this Pharaoh was. Some are of the opinion that he was Thotmes III (fifteenth century B.C.E.), and others, Rameses II (thirteenth century B.C.E.).

Over the years, the Israelites had grown into a nation of almost two million people. Pharaoh feared their growing strength because, if war came, they might join the enemy and cause his overthrow. So he forced them into slavery, and had them dragged away from their homes to work in the fields, and build cities and fortresses, under the supervision of cruel task-masters. Two of these cities were called Pithom and Raamses, near the Egyptian frontier, where food and military equipment were stored for defence purposes. Pharaoh's plans to weaken the Israelites failed for, in spite of all their suffering, they continued to increase in number. His next step was to order the Hebrew midwives to kill every male child at birth, but fearing God, they disobeyed him. Finally, Pharaoh commanded that every newborn son should be drowned in the river Nile.

Pharaoh's daughter adopts a Hebrew child

It was at this critical moment in Israel's history that their future liberator was born. Amram and Jochebed of the tribe of Levi already had two children, Miriam and Aaron, and soon after the king's cruel decree a second son was born. After hiding the child carefully for three months, his mother put him in an ark of bulrushes among the reeds on the banks of the river Nile, leaving Miriam to watch over it at a distance. One day, Pharaoh's daughter came down to bathe, saw the ark and sent one of her maidservants to bring it to her. She realized that it was a Hebrew child and, touched with pity, decided to adopt it. Miriam came forward and, with the princess's permission to find a nurse, brought back the child's real mother. Jochebed looked after her son for a few years and taught him the traditions of his ancestors. Later he was taken to the royal palace and given the name of Moses, which means 'drawn out of the water'. Moses received his education at the Egyptian court but never forgot his Hebrew origin, and was greatly troubled by his people's misery and suffering.

Moses punishes a cruel taskmaster, and flees to Midian

Moses was forty years old when something happened which altered the whole course of his life. He often visited his fellow Israelites working in the labour camps and, one day, saw an Egyptian overseer beating one of the slaves. Moses could not bear the sight of such cruelty and, thinking they were alone, killed the Egyptian and buried his body in the sand. On the following day, when he intervened in a quarrel between two Israelites, the aggressor was sarcastic and asked what right Moses had to interfere. Did he intend killing him also? Moses realized the secret was out and that as soon as Pharaoh heard the news he would sentence him to death. So he fled to the land of Midian, in the south-eastern region of the Sinai Peninsula. He reached a well near one of the cities and drove away some shepherds who were preventing the seven daughters of Jethro, the priest of Midian, from drawing water for their sheep. When Jethro heard of this gallant act, he invited Moses to stay with him and look after his flocks. Moses accepted and afterwards married Jethro's daughter Zipporah, by whom he had two sons, Gershom and Eliezer. Although he, himself, was safe and happy, Moses never ceased grieving for his fellow Israelites.

21

Moses is chosen by God to rescue the Israelites

Nearly forty years had passed since Moses fled from Egypt. Although the cruel Pharaoh had died, the oppression continued with even greater severity under his successor. One day, whilst tending Jethro's flocks near the mountain-range of Horeb, in the Sinai Peninsula, Moses saw a strange sight. A thorn bush was in flames yet the dry branches were not consumed by the fire. As he turned aside to gaze at this wonder, Moses heard God's voice directing him not to come nearer the bush, but to take his shoes off, for the place on which he stood was holy ground. Then God called on Moses to deliver the Israelites from bondage and lead them to the Land of Promise. Moses, a man of great modesty, pleaded that he was unworthy, but God assured him that He would be with him. Moses was to tell the elders of Israel of this Divine revelation, and together they were to demand of Pharaoh that he allow the people to undertake a three-day journey into the wilderness to sacrifice to God.

When Moses protested that the people would not believe him, God gave him the power to perform three miracles: (a) his rod changed into a serpent when thrown on the ground, but resumed its original form when the serpent was seized by the tail; (b) his hand became leprous when withdrawn from his bosom, but healed completely when he put it back in his bosom and withdrew it a second time; (c) and if a third sign were to prove necessary, Moses was to pour water from the river Nile on to the dry land and it would turn into blood. Moses still hesitated as he lacked eloquence and was slow of speech, but God told him that Aaron his brother would be his spokesman. Moses was now convinced that he had been chosen by God to liberate His people and, with Jethro's permission, began his journey to Egypt.

Moses challenges Pharaoh

Moses met Aaron at Mount Horeb, and together they returned to Egypt. When the people heard the account of the Divine message, and saw the miraculous signs, they were confident that God had seen their affliction and they all bowed down in worship before Him.

Fearlessly the two brothers arrived at the palace and, appearing before Pharaoh, requested him to let the Israelites leave Egypt and hold a feast to God in the wilderness. Not only did Pharaoh refuse, but he treated the people even more

22

harshly. They were no longer to be supplied with straw, which held the clay together, yet the same number of bricks was to be made. The Hebrew foremen, who worked under the Egyptian taskmasters, were flogged because they could not carry out such an impossible task. Their appeal to the king for mercy was rejected, so they turned angrily against Moses and Aaron. In reply to Moses' complaint that his mission had failed, God assured him that Pharaoh, after being severely punished for his wickedness, would be compelled by His might to free the people.

Moses was eighty years old and Aaron eighty-three when they again appeared before Pharaoh and renewed their request. Knowing that the king would be impressed with a miraculous sign, Aaron threw down his rod before him and it turned into a serpent. The Egyptian magicians were able to imitate this wonder and even though Aaron's rod swallowed up their rods, Pharaoh hardened his heart and refused to let the people go.

Ten Plagues break down Pharaoh's resistance

Through his arrogance and defiance, Pharaoh brought the most terrible calamities upon himself and his people. God's power made itself felt by the infliction of nine plagues, one after the other, the worst in human history. They occurred in this order: (i) The river Nile and all the waters of Egypt turned into blood; (ii) there was an invasion of frogs over the land; (iii) gnats sprang in their hundreds of thousands from the dust of the dry land; (iv) swarms of insects invaded the Egyptian homes; (v) a cattle plague killed most of the Egyptian horses, herds and flocks; (vi) an epidemic of boils broke out among men and animals; (vii) a torrential hailstorm caused havoc among the crops; (viii) the dreaded locust devoured the entire vegetation; (ix) thick darkness covered the land for three days, and the people were terrified to move out of their homes.

Pharaoh was given the opportunity to relent, but once the danger had passed, he remained as stubborn as ever, until the dense gloom and confusion resulting from the ninth plague proved too much for him. He now offered to allow the children to accompany their parents and worship God, provided the flocks and herds were left behind as security for their return. Moses refused and was forbidden by Pharaoh to appear before him again under pain of death. God had already told Moses that the final plague was to be brought upon Pharaoh, forcing him to yield, and, in preparation for their departure, the Israelites were to ask for gifts of silver and jewels from the Egyptians. Moses, in reply to the king's final word, warned him that all the first-born of Egypt, men and cattle, would die at midnight and that the king's courtiers would beg the Israelites to leave.

The first Passover is observed

Before the final blow was struck, the Israelites were commanded to commemorate for all time the historic event they were about to witness. On the tenth day of the first month (Nisan), each householder set aside an unblemished lamb or kid of the first year, slaughtered it on the evening of the fourteenth day, and sprinkled its blood on the doorposts of their homes. That night, the flesh was eaten roasted, together with unleavened bread and bitter herbs. The meal was consumed in haste and the children of Israel were suitably dressed in preparation for a journey. At midnight, God struck down all the Egyptian first-born, men and cattle, but passed over those houses sprinkled with the blood. From every home the sound of bitter weeping could be heard and Pharaoh's stubborn resistance was broken. He and the Egyptians begged the Israelites to leave at once, giving them as much silver, gold and garments as they requested. The Israelites, having no time to leaven their dough, took it with them in their kneading troughs. On the fifteenth day of Nisan, some two million men, women and children left the land of slavery and began their long march towards the land of freedom. In celebration of this epoch-making event, and in accordance with God's command, the festival of Passover has been observed ever since for a period of seven days, during which no leaven may be eaten.

Moses did not forget the pledge given by his ancestors (see page 19), and ordered Joseph's remains to be carried out of Egypt for burial in the Promised Land.

The Israelites cross the Red Sea

The nearest route to Canaan lay along the coast through the land of the powerful and warlike Philistines. As this would have involved the Israelites in an immediate battle for which they were totally unprepared, Moses led them from Raamses on the Egyptian frontier, in a south-easterly direction. They were guided by a pillar of cloud during the day and by a pillar

24

of fire at night. After a few days, they encamped near the northern arm of the Red Sea known today as the Gulf of Suez.

As soon as Pharaoh had recovered from the shock caused by the death of the first-born, he regretted his decision to release his former slaves. Assembling his army, he followed in hot pursuit. When the Israelites saw the advancing army in the distance, they panicked and complained bitterly to Moses. 'It would have been better to serve in Egypt than die in the wilderness', they cried, but Moses assured them that God would fight for them. The guiding pillar of cloud moved to their rear, and hindered the Egyptian advance. Moses, at God's bidding, stretched out his hand over the Red Sea and a strong east wind blew all that night, dividing the waters. The next day the Israelites crossed the sea on dry land with the waters forming a wall on either side, and reached the opposite bank safe and sound. The pursuers drove on to the sea-bed and their chariot wheels became embedded in the sand. To add to their troubles, a raging storm burst over their heads and threw them into confusion. The Egyptians realized that disaster was at hand and attempted to turn back, but it was too late, for Moses stretched out his hand over the sea. The waters rushed back and resumed their normal course, engulfing the entire Egyptian army. A triumphant song was sung by Moses and the Children of Israel, in which they praised God's power in destroying the enemy. Miriam, too, led the women in singing God's praises.

The Israelites are miraculously supplied with food and water

The Israelites continued their journey through the wilderness of Shur, to a place called Marah (i.e., bitterness), so called because of its bitter waters. Parched with thirst, the people murmured against Moses. At the Divine command, he threw the branch of a certain type of shrub into the waters, which made them sweet and drinkable without causing any ill-effects. After the people had quenched their thirst, they moved on to the oasis of Elim.

Proceeding inland, they entered the Sinai wilderness, one month after their departure from Egypt. Soon, the lack of food made them wish they had never left, but their hunger was satisfied when, in the evening, birds known as quails descended on the camp. In the morning, the ground was covered with manna, a sugary substance which tasted like honey-cake. Each

25

Israelite was commanded to gather no more than an omer (a measure of just under four pints) every day, but a double portion was gathered on the sixth day, to provide food for the Sabbath. An omer of manna was later placed in an earthenware pot and preserved before the Ark in the Tabernacle. The manna continued to appear throughout the wanderings in the wilderness until the crossing of the river Jordan (see page 46).

In Rephidim, further south, the people again grumbled at the lack of water. At God's bidding, Moses struck a rock at the nearby Mount Horeb with the rod he had used in Egypt, and streams of water gushed forth. The place where this happened was called Massah ('testing' God) and Meribah ('strife').

The Amalekites attack the marching column

The first great battle was waged at Rephidim when the Amalekites harassed the marching columns by attacking the stragglers. The Israelites fought back, led by Joshua, the son of Nun, whilst Moses watched from the peak of a hill, holding up his rod. He was accompanied by Aaron and Hur, who supported his hands when he became tired, for the Israelites, inspired by the sight of their leader with his hands uplifted, fought with greater confidence. At sunset, Amalek was utterly defeated and Moses wrote an account of this act of treachery to remind Joshua, who was to succeed him, that the tribe of Amalek was to be completely destroyed.

Jethro pays Moses a visit

While Moses was carrying out his mission in Egypt, his family had returned to Midian. Jethro now brought his daughter Zipporah, Moses' wife, and their two sons to Rephidim. Moses received Jethro with respect and affection and told him of God's miraculous deeds. His father-in-law joyfully acknowledged God's power and offered sacrifices to Him. Seeing how Moses, apart from his other tasks, was overburdened with legal duties, Jethro advised him to deal only with the more difficult cases, and to refer the others to assistant judges. Moses acted on his advice and Jethro returned to Midian.

Readings from
the Bible

Exodus, chapter 2, verses 1 to 10   Pharaoh's daughter adopts Moses
Exodus, chapter 3   Call of Moses
Exodus, chapter 12, verses 1 to 20   The Passover
Exodus, chapter 14, verses 15 to 31   Crossing of the Red Sea

Exercises

1. Explain why Moses was worthy of being chosen by God to liberate the Israelites.
2. 'And they shall eat the flesh in that night, roast with fire, and unleavened bread; with bitter herbs they shall eat it' (Exodus, chapter 12, verse 8). What were the reasons for this commandment?
3. Imagine you were one of the Israelites who had just left Egypt. Describe, in your own words, the Egyptian pursuit and the crossing of the Red Sea.
4. Write briefly on the following:
   (*a*) Raamses; (*b*) Marah; (*c*) Meribah; (*d*) Rephidim.

5

MOUNT SINAI

Moses receives the Ten Commandments on Mount Sinai

ON the first day of the third month after they had left Egypt, the Children of Israel arrived in the wilderness of Sinai and encamped before the mountain range on which God had revealed Himself to Moses at the burning bush. Moses went up to the summit of Mount Sinai and brought back several Divine messages. He told the Israelites they had been chosen to become 'a kingdom of priests and a holy nation' provided they obeyed God's commandments. With one voice, the people declared, 'All that the Lord has spoken we will do'. Moses then revealed to them that in another three days God would appear in a thick cloud and speak to him before the whole assembly. The people were to prepare themselves for this great event, and were not to touch the boundaries round the mountain under penalty of death.

After these three days had passed, amid thunder and lightning, the sound of the trumpet was heard and Moses brought the people to the foot of the mountain. Mount Sinai was covered by a dense cloud and God called Moses to its summit. Then followed the greatest event the world has ever known. The voice of God, proclaiming the Ten Commandments, was heard by every man, woman, and child gathered round Mount Sinai. The people were so terrified by this experience that they withdrew some distance from the mountain and pleaded with Moses to speak to them in God's place. Moses approached the thick darkness and received a number of laws which he wrote down and read to the people who, without hesitation, accepted

28

the responsibilities imposed upon them. Moses was then called up alone to receive from God the two tablets of stone on which the Ten Commandments were inscribed. Followed by Joshua, who remained on the lower part of the mountain, Moses ascended Mount Sinai, where he stayed for forty days, and received further revelations.

The Israelites worship the golden calf

During Moses' long absence, the people became impatient and, fearing that he would never return, demanded a leader that they could see and worship. Knowing how hasty they were, Aaron fashioned a calf out of their golden ear-rings. The people brought sacrifices to their idol, around which they sang and danced, calling out, 'This is thy god, O Israel'. God's anger was aroused and He sent Moses down from the mount telling him of Israel's sin, and declaring that He would destroy this treacherous people. Moses begged God to be merciful and not to give the Egyptians the opportunity of gloating over the Israelites' misfortune, but to recall His covenant with the Patriarchs.

Descending from the mountain and accompanied by Joshua, Moses heard the cries of revelry, witnessed the disgraceful behaviour of the people, and, in anger, dashed the tablets of stone to the ground. He then seized the calf, burnt it with fire, and mixed its ashes with water, which he made the people drink. After reproaching Aaron, who pleaded that he had been forced to carry out the people's demands, Moses called on all his supporters to rally round him, and the Levites made an immediate response — at his command they went through the camp, killing about three thousand ringleaders.

The second Tablets of Stone

In spite of this terrible lapse into idolatry, Moses' love and compassion for his people led him to obtain God's pardon for their sin. Again Moses went up alone into the mountain taking with him two other tablets of stone which God had commanded him to bring. After spending another forty days on the mountain during which he neither ate nor drank, Moses returned to the camp carrying the tablets of stone inscribed with the Ten Commandments, and communicated all the laws he had received on Mount Sinai to Aaron, the elders, and the whole assembly.

Plans are prepared
for the erection of
the Sanctuary

For almost a year, the Israelites encamped in the nearby mountain. During this period, they were taught by Moses to understand and observe the Divine laws, and lead an upright life.* So that they should always be aware of God's presence in their midst, the people were commanded to build a Sanctuary. Willingly and generously they brought free-will offerings of precious metals and brass, fabrics and skins of various kinds, wood, oil, spices and incense as well as precious stones. Women with the necessary skill spun the linen material and even gave their mirrors of burnished copper to be used for the making of the laver (a large vessel in which the priests could wash) and its base. All the work was supervised by Bezalel, of the tribe of Judah, a man of wisdom and experience, assisted by Oholiab, of the tribe of Dan, who was a skilled engraver and weaver. Contributions poured in to such an extent that the workmen reported to Moses they had more than they needed, so the people were told to stop bringing them.

The Sanctuary and
its contents

The Sanctuary consisted of an outer Court, which the laymen could enter, and the Tabernacle, divided by a curtain into two parts: The Holy Place, where the priest performed many of his sacred duties, and the Holy of Holies, which the High Priest alone entered once a year on the Day of Atonement.

The Sanctuary was a roofless oblong enclosure measuring about one hundred and fifty feet by seventy-five feet and was constructed of boards of acacia wood covered by layers of curtains. In the outer court stood the altar of burnt-offering and the laver or basin, in which the priests washed before they performed their duties.

The Holy Place was thirty feet long and fifteen feet wide and high. It contained the golden Menorah with its seven lamps, the altar of incense and the table of showbread, on which twelve loaves were placed fresh each Sabbath by the priests, who then ate the old loaves within the precincts of the Sanctuary.

The Holy of Holies formed a perfect cube, being fifteen feet in length, width and height. In it stood nothing but the Ark

* These laws require careful study. According to an early Jewish tradition, 613 commandments were revealed to Moses, and it is obviously impossible to deal with them adequately in this book. The reader is referred to the author's companion volume 'Introduction to Judaism', in which many of the laws applying to our daily life are explained in some detail.

containing the two tablets of stone. The Ark measured three feet nine inches long and was two feet three inches wide and deep. It was made of acacia wood, and was overlaid by a plate of solid gold screened by the wings of two cherubim facing each other on either side.

The Priests and Levites are chosen to serve in the Sanctuary

The tribe of Levi, which had rallied round Moses after the incident of the Golden Calf (see page 29) was chosen to carry out the duties associated with the Sanctuary. Aaron and his sons, Nadab, Abihu, Eleazar, and Ithamar, were specially selected to serve as priests. The other Levites acted as their assistants and their main task was to transport the Sanctuary and its contents from place to place. The office of High Priest was conferred on Aaron, who wore the distinctive garment known as the Ephod. Attached to the Ephod was the Breastplate of Judgment, on which were set twelve precious stones in four rows, each engraved with the name of one of the tribes.

Nadab and Abihu are punished for their sin

The Sanctuary was erected under Moses' personal supervision, on the first day of the first month (Nisan), nine months after the arrival at Sinai. In an impressive ceremony lasting seven days, Aaron and his sons were consecrated and installed by Moses as priests in the presence of the congregation. The joyous occasion was suddenly marred by a tragic incident. Aaron's eldest sons, Nadab and Abihu, offered up incense on unconsecrated fire not taken from the altar. Such an offence by priests who were to set an example to the people was unpardonable, and they were punished by instant death 'by fire which came from before the Lord'. Aaron was overwhelmed with grief but, consoled by his brother Moses, resigned himself to God's will.

The Israelites had been at Sinai for almost a year. The Ten Commandments and the Divine laws had been proclaimed, the Sanctuary had been erected, and the priests consecrated. The time had come to continue the journey towards Canaan.

Readings from
the Bible

Exodus, chapter 20, verses 1 to 14   The Ten Commandments
Exodus, chapter 32   The golden calf
Exodus, chapter 25, verses 1 to 9,
   Exodus, chapter 35, verses 20 to 29
   and chapter 36, verses 2 to 7   The Tabernacle

Exercises

1. Trace, on a map, the route taken so far by the Israelites in the peninsula of Sinai.
2. Learn the Ten Commandments by heart, and read chapter 19 of the Book of Leviticus. Can you see any connection between these two Biblical passages?
3. Make a list of the articles in the Sanctuary, and write a short note on each.
4. Why was Aaron chosen to be the first High Priest?

6

IN THE WILDERNESS

The Israelites leave Sinai

ON the first day of the second month (Iyyar), in the second year after the Exodus, the Israelites were commanded to continue their march towards Canaan. The camp was arranged as a quadrilateral, with the Tabernacle, which was in the centre, protected on all four sides by the Levites' tents. The twelve tribes were divided into four sections, each bearing the name of its leading tribe, which formed the outer cordon. Judah, together with Issachar and Zebulun, were stationed on the east; Reuben, with Simeon and Gad on the south; Ephraim, with Manasseh and Benjamin on the west; and Dan, with Asher and Naphtali on the north. When on the march, the contingent of Judah took the lead followed by Reuben and Ephraim, with Dan in the rear. Moses urged Jethro, his father-in-law, to act as a guide on the journey, but he refused, as he preferred to remain in his native land, Midian.

The following four incidents illustrate some of the difficulties with which Moses was now faced.

At Taberah

(i) Shortly after leaving Sinai, the people complained bitterly of the harsh conditions to which they were exposed. Because of their lack of faith in the Divine Promise, they were punished by an outbreak of fire which caused considerable damage. It subsided only after Moses had prayed to God on the people's behalf. The place of this occurrence was, after this, known as Taberah ('burning').

33

(ii) On another occasion, demands for meat and food came from the foreigners who had escaped from Egyptian bondage with the Israelites, for they had become tired of the manna which was their staple diet. Moses felt that the responsibility of governing the people was too much for him and in despair asked for God's help. He was told to assemble seventy elders at the Sanctuary who would share his burden and upon whom God would bestow part of the Divine spirit resting on Moses. The elders, whom Moses selected, stood near the Sanctuary and, seized with the feeling of spiritual ecstasy, began to prophesy. Two of them, named Eldad and Medad, had not responded to Moses' summons and remained in the camp. They, too, felt the urge to prophesy even though they had not come out to the Sanctuary. Moses was informed, and Joshua, full of zeal for his master's authority, asked him to restrain them. But Moses showed true greatness by replying, 'Would that all the Lord's people were prophets, that the Lord would put His spirit upon them'.

(iii) The wind brought an abundance of quails from across the sea, and the people displayed such gluttony that they fell upon the food. This time, their greed was punished by the outbreak of a plague. The place where this occurred was called Kibroth — hattaavah ('the graves of lust').

(iv) At Hazeroth, the next halting place, Miriam and Aaron spoke ill of Moses because he had married an Ethiopian woman, and claimed equal authority with him since they, too, had received Divine inspiration. Moses, a man of great humility, remained silent, but God descended in a pillar of cloud and called Aaron and Miriam to the Tabernacle where He rebuked them. Though Divine revelations were sometimes made to other prophets through visions or dreams, Moses' position was unique since he was the only person to whom God directly revealed His will. When the cloud departed, Miriam was inflicted with leprosy, and Aaron, after confessing his error, pleaded with Moses for their sister's recovery. Miriam, although healed as a result of Moses' prayer, was isolated for seven days outside the camp.

After this the Israelites moved on to the wilderness of Paran.

*Twelve spies report
on conditions in
Canaan*

The Israelites had reached Kadesh Barnea in the wilderness of Paran, at the very gate of the Promised Land. Twelve men, leaders of their respective tribes, were sent by Moses to explore Canaan and report back on the condition of its people, vegetation and fortifications. Joshua, of the tribe of Ephraim, and Caleb, of the tribe of Judah, were among those selected. The spies secretly crossed the mountain path of the Negev in southern Canaan and penetrated the land to the extreme north. After an absence of forty days they returned, bringing with them clusters of grapes, pomegranates and figs as evidence of

The twelve spies return from Canaan

the land's fertility. They maintained, however, that it would be impossible to conquer Canaan as it was inhabited by strong and powerful men, and the cities were strongly fortified. Caleb, followed by Joshua, was more optimistic than they were and urged an immediate attack. The people sided with the majority and, panic-stricken, broke out into open rebellion. They wanted to elect a leader to lead them back to Egypt. They refused to listen to the renewed pleas of Caleb and Joshua, and threatened to stone them to death.

In anger, God communicated to Moses His intention of destroying the people and of forming a new nation from Moses' own descendants. Once again Moses pleaded on their behalf, and was told that the Israelites should turn back into the wilderness in the direction of the Red Sea and not attempt any attack on the inhabitants of Canaan. Although total destruction was averted, it was decreed that the people should wander in the wilderness for forty years — a year for each day the spies had searched the land — until all over the age of twenty, with the exception of Caleb and Joshua, had died. The next generation would enter the Promised Land to witness the fulfilment of God's promise.

The ten spies died as a result of a sudden plague. Too late, the people realized their guilt and declared their intention of making an immediate attack on Canaan, ignoring Moses' warning against this further defiance of God's will. Their attack ended in disaster, for, heavily defeated by the Amalekites and Canaanites, they suffered severe losses and were driven back to Hormah, about twenty-five miles north-east of Kadesh.

Korah leads a rebellion against Moses

Moses' troubles were by no means at an end. A group of Levites led by Korah, who was a cousin of Moses and Aaron, and a group of Reubenites led by Dathan, Abiram and On, were joined by two hundred and fifty prominent but discontented laymen in revolt against Moses and Aaron. Korah considered he had as much right as Aaron to be elevated to the High Priesthood. Dathan and his associates wished to take Moses' place and based their claim to the leadership on their descent from Reuben, the first-born of Jacob. Moses challenged Korah and his followers to appear next day at the Sanctuary before God, with censers filled with incense, and God Himself would show whom He had chosen.

Korah and his associates, followed by many sympathisers, appeared next day at the Sanctuary to undergo the test. Dathan and Abiram, however, refused to attend. Moses, having warned the people to stand aloof from the tents of Korah, Dathan and Abiram, announced the test by which the true leadership would be decided. If the rebels died a natural death then Moses would be proved in the wrong; if, however, the earth swallowed them alive, it would prove that they had despised God.

No sooner had Moses spoken than Korah and the other rebels with all their possessions perished in an earthquake and the people fled in terror. In addition, the two hundred and fifty men who offered incense were destroyed by fire. Their censers were collected by Eleazar the priest and made into plates for the covering of the Altar of burnt-offering, as a warning that only Aaron and his descendants were permitted to burn incense before the Lord. The people turned against Moses and Aaron whom they held responsible for the death of so many of their leaders, and were punished by a plague. Moses told Aaron to take a censer of fire and incense from the Altar, move among the people and pray that they should be forgiven. The plague

36

then ceased, but not before nearly fifteen thousand people had died.

Aaron's position as High Priest is confirmed

The princes of the twelve tribes were each commanded to bring a rod, inscribed with their names. These, together with the rod of Levi, bearing the name of Aaron, were deposited before the Ark. The following morning Aaron's rod alone was found to have produced buds, blossoms and almonds — a clear sign that God had chosen him to be High Priest. Aaron's rod was preserved before the Ark as a warning to future generations never again to challenge his right to the priesthood.

Moses and Aaron disobey God's command

For thirty-eight years the Israelites roamed through the wilderness, probably making Kadesh their headquarters. During this long period, most of the older generation died. In the first month of the fortieth year after the Exodus, the new generation assembled at Kadesh. History repeated itself when the people again complained of thirst. God told Moses and Aaron to speak to the rock from which enough water would come to satisfy the thirst of the people. In anger at the people's constant rebelliousness, Moses impatiently struck the rock twice instead, and water flowed. Because they had not believed and honoured God before the people, Moses and Aaron were told that they would not be permitted to enter the Holy Land. The waters were named Meribah (strife), recalling a similar incident many years before (see page 26). While the Israelites were still encamped at Kadesh, Miriam died and was buried there.

The king of Edom blocks the Israelites' advance

The people were now told to prepare for the last stages of their journey. Having failed to enter Canaan from the south (see page 36), there was no alternative but to journey eastwards through the land of Edom, south of the Dead Sea. Moses sent messengers to the king of Edom, requesting permission to cross his territory, and offering to pay for any water the people and cattle might drink. Not only did the king refuse, but he barred the way with an armed force, and the Israelites were compelled to take the roundabout route by the southern borders of Edom. When they reached Mount Hor, a peak in the range of Mount Seir, Aaron died and was buried there, and Moses installed Eleazar as the next High Priest.

All resistance is overcome, and eastern Jordan is conquered

After successfully driving off an attack by the Canaanite king of Arad, the people, weary and discouraged, complained bitterly of their plight and of the lack of food and water. They were punished with a plague of fiery serpents. When they repented, Moses was told to set a serpent made of brass upon a pole — whoever had been bitten was healed when he looked at it. This symbol was preserved right up to the time of Hezekiah, who destroyed it (see page 143). The journey which had taken them south, east and then north around the lands of Edom and Moab came to a halt when they reached the river Arnon, the boundary between the Moabites in the south and the Amorites in the north.

Sihon, king of the Amorites, refused to allow the Israelites to pass through his land and led his army against them, but the battle ended with the utter defeat of the Amorite ruler, and his territory was captured. Turning northwards towards the fertile lands of Gilead and Bashan, the Israelites overcame the resistance of Og, king of Bashan, at the battle of Edrei, and took possession of his country which extended as far as Mount Hermon in the north. The land on the east side of the Jordan had been captured, and the Israelites finally encamped on the borders of Moab facing Jericho, making their headquarters at the city of Shittim.

————————➤•⊂————————

Readings from the Bible

Numbers, chapter 11, verses 16, 17, 24 to 29   Eldad and Medad prophesy

Numbers, chapter 13   The twelve spies

Numbers, chapter 16   Korah's rebellion

Exercises

1. Trace the route taken by the Israelites from Egypt to the borders of Moab.
2. Draw a sketch of the Israelite camp, showing where each of the tribes was stationed.
3. Imagine you were one of the twelve spies. Describe your impressions of Canaan.
4. No representative of the tribe of Levi was sent by Moses to explore Canaan. Can you suggest the reason?
5. Write briefly on the following:
   (*a*) Hazeroth; (*b*) Aaron's rod; (*c*) Kadesh.

7

IN THE PLAINS OF MOAB

Balak bribes Balaam to curse the Israelites

BALAK, king of Moab, was alarmed at the Israelites' victory over the Amorites and, dreading an invasion of his own country, made an alliance with the Midianites. The king decided to approach Balaam, a famous heathen soothsayer of Pethor, on the river Euphrates, to curse the Israelites. The invitation was conveyed in person by elders of Moab and Midian who brought gifts with them. Balaam asked the delegation to remain overnight as he wished to consult God. During the night he was warned not to go with them and curse the people, so he sent the men away.

Thinking that a more tempting offer would have the desired effect, Balak sent a second delegation, more numerous and of higher rank, who offered even greater honours and reward. Balaam asked them to remain overnight so that he could again seek guidance. This time he was given permission to go but to speak only as God would direct him. During the journey his ass, seeing an angel with drawn sword barring the way, turned aside. Balaam struck the animal several times and the ass miraculously spoke out in protest at such cruelty. Then Balaam himself saw the angel who told him he was at fault for accepting Balak's invitation. The soothsayer offered to turn back but was again instructed to continue his journey and to speak only God's message.

Balaam praises the Israelites

Balak met Balaam at the river Arnon and brought him to a nearby city where he held a feast in his honour. The next day, Balaam was taken to a hill sacred to the god Baal, from which

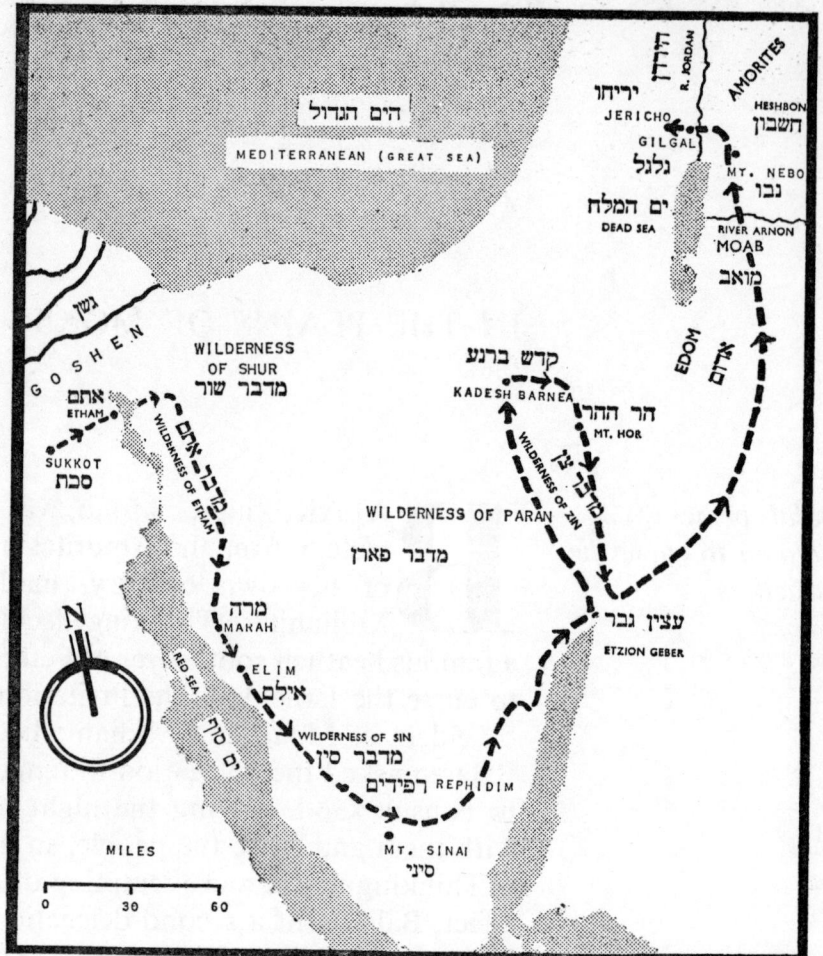

Map labels:

הים הגדול
MEDITERRANEAN (GREAT SEA)

ירדן
R. JORDAN

AMORITES

יריחו
JERICHO

חשבון
HESHBON

גלגל
GILGAL

מט. נבו
MT. NEBO
נבו

ים המלח
DEAD SEA

RIVER ARNON
MOAB
מואב

גשן
GOSHEN

אתם
ETHAM

WILDERNESS OF SHUR
מדבר שור

WILDERNESS OF ETHAM

סכת
SUKKOT

קדש ברנע
KADESH BARNEA

הר ההר
MT. HOR

EDOM

אדום

WILDERNESS OF ZIN

מרה
MARAH

WILDERNESS OF PARAN
מדבר פארן

עצין גבר
ETZION GEBER

אילם
ELIM

RED SEA

ים סוף

WILDERNESS OF SIN
מדבר סין
רפידים
REPHIDIM

מט. סיני
MT. SINAI
סיני

N

MILES

0   30   60

Wandering of the Israelites

he could see part of the Israelite camp. After king and prophet
had sacrificed a bullock and a ram on each of seven altars,
Balaam withdrew some distance to find out God's wishes.
On his return, he delivered his first prophecy. 'How', asked
Balaam, 'could he curse those whom God had not cursed?
Israel was a nation distinguished from other peoples and had
become a mighty multitude.' Angered at Balaam's words of
praise, Balak took him to the top of Mount Pisgah, where the
same ceremonies were repeated but with the same result.
Balaam declared that God would not break His promise to
bless Israel, who, with His help, were delivered from Egypt —
no magic could prevail against them. Balak, in despair, told
Balaam neither to bless nor curse them.

40

Balak made yet a third attempt, and took Balaam to the top of Mount Peor, overlooking the desert. The seven-fold sacrifice was repeated, but on this occasion Balaam did not withdraw as before. He could only express his delight at the tranquillity and contentment enjoyed by the Israelites — 'How goodly are thy tents, O Jacob, Thy dwellings, O Israel!' Such a people, he concluded, was destined to become great and victorious.

In a rage, Balak dismissed the prophet but, before departing, Balaam foretold the sovereignty of Israel and the doom of Moab, Edom, Amalek and the mighty Assyrian empire.

Phinehas sets an example

Balaam did not return to Pethor but incited the heathen women of Moab and Midian to tempt the Israelites to join in the worship of Baal-Peor, one of the Moabite gods. Phinehas, the son of Eleazar the High Priest, set an example of zeal by executing Zimri, a Simeonite prince, and Cozbi, a Midianite princess, for practising idolatry openly before the whole people. As a reward, he was promised that the priesthood would always be retained by his descendants.

Balaam is killed in the battle against Midian

The Israelites were ordered to launch an attack against the Midianites and punish them for their disgraceful conduct. In the battle which followed, the five rulers of Midian as well as the false soothsayer, Balaam, were killed. The booty was divided equally between the soldiers and those who had remained behind. One five-hundredth of their share was paid by the soldiers for the benefit of the priests, whereas one fiftieth of the non-combatants' share went to the Levites. The returning victors, thankful that not one of them had died in battle, made an additional freewill offering to the Sanctuary of the golden ornaments they had captured.

Moses appoints Joshua as his successor

God commanded Moses to ascend the mountain range of Abarim and view the Promised Land before his death. Moses' immediate concern was for his people, and he asked that his successor be appointed without delay. God directed him to lay his hand upon Joshua, signifying the transference of his authority, and to present him to Eleazar, the priest, as well as to the whole congregation, and publicly confer on him the dignity of office.

Moses also entrusted Joshua with the task of dividing the land of Canaan, once it had been conquered, among the tribes, on the principle that the bigger the tribe, the more land it would get. Its geographical position would be decided by the casting of lots. No separate territory was to be allotted to the Levites who had the special and sacred task of ministering in the Sanctuary and acting as teachers and guides to the people. They were, however, to receive forty-eight cities with their suburbs on both sides of the Jordan. Six of these Levitical cities were to be set aside as Cities of Refuge, three on either side of the Jordan, to provide asylum for a man who killed another accidentally. His life was to be spared, but he had to remain in the city until the death of the High Priest, and could then return to his family.

The two and a half tribes ask for special privileges

The tribes of Reuben and Gad possessed large herds of cattle, and sought permission to settle in the pasture territory of Gilead, on the east of the Jordan. At first Moses disapproved, as he feared that if they were to remain behind, the other tribes would lose heart and there might be a repetition of what happened after the return of the twelve spies. The Reubenites and Gadites explained that they fully intended to cross the Jordan and join the others in the conquest of Canaan, leaving behind only their families and cattle in fortified cities. Moses now yielded and charged Joshua to see that the promise was fulfilled. The same privilege was given to part of the tribe of Manasseh, which had taken an active part in the conquest of Gilead.

Moses delivers three farewell addresses

In the eleventh month of the fortieth year after the Exodus, Moses delivered three farewell addresses to the new generation about to enter the Promised Land. In them, he reviewed the events of the past, repeated many important laws, and gave guidance for the future. He repeatedly stressed the importance of observing the commandments and the dreadful consequences of idol worship and of imitating the hideous rites of the Canaanites.

Moses set down the law in writing, delivered it to the priests and elders and instructed them to have it read publicly on the Feast of Tabernacles, at the end of each seventh year, to the

42

Israelites assembled at the Central Sanctuary. In this way, man, woman and child would hear, study and observe the teachings of the Torah. The Book of the Law was placed by the Levites beside the Ark to bear witness against Israel if they should ever disobey its teachings.

Moses' death

Before his death, Moses pronounced a blessing on Israel. In poetical language he described the revelation of God to His people at Sinai when He gave them the Law. Then, blessing each of the tribes in turn, Moses foretold their future happiness and prosperity, and concluded with praise of God who protected the people, providing them with security and comfort.

The life of the great leader was nearing its end, but though he was one hundred and twenty years old he was in full possession of all his faculties. Moses went up from the plains of Moab to Mount Nebo, the summit of Pisgah. Alone with God, he was shown from afar all the territory which would one day be the homeland of the people of Israel. So Moses, the servant of the Lord, died in the land of Moab and was buried in the valley, 'but no man knows of his burial place unto this day'. The people mourned the loss of their leader for thirty days and then turned to Joshua, his successor.

Readings from the Bible

Numbers, chapter 22	The story of Balaam
Numbers, chapter 27, verses 12 to 23	Moses appoints Joshua as his successor
Numbers, chapter 32	The two and a half tribes
Deuteronomy, chapter 34	Moses' death

Exercises

1. Mention six important events which occurred during the wanderings in the wilderness. Write more fully on two of them.
2. Describe the conquest of the eastern side of the Jordan.
3. Why is Moses considered the greatest of all the prophets?
4. On what occasions were the following said, and by whom?
   (*a*) Come now, therefore, I pray thee, curse me this people.
   (*b*) Let the Lord, the God of the spirits of all flesh, set a man over the congregation.
   (*c*) Shall your brethren go to the war and shall ye sit here?

8

THE CONQUEST OF CANAAN

Joshua plans his campaign

AFTER the death of Moses, Joshua, the son of Nun of the tribe of Ephraim, was faced with the tremendous responsibility of invading the land of Canaan and of overcoming, by degrees, the strong resistance of the numerous tribes inhabiting the land.

There could be little doubt that Joshua was equal to the task, for already during Moses' lifetime he had proved himself not only courageous and determined but also a man of deep faith and loyalty. Let us briefly recall some of the incidents in the earlier phase of his career. He had led the army against the attack of the Amalekites and utterly defeated the enemy (see page 26); had accompanied Moses to the foot of Mount Sinai before Moses received the two tablets of stone (see page 29); upheld his master's authority in the incident of Eldad and Medad (see page 34); opposed, with Caleb, the defeatist attitude of the other ten spies (see page 35); had been appointed Moses' successor during his leader's lifetime (see page 41); and had been given the task of dividing the land of Canaan fairly among the twelve tribes (see page 42).

There is sufficient historical evidence to show that Canaan had already been overrun by the Egyptians who made the numerous city-states, each of which had its own petty independent king, pay them money as tribute. However, the Egyptian rulers were by this time busy with home affairs and could not spare troops for the defence of satellite countries.

Joshua, inspired by the word of God 'to be strong and of good courage', began to prepare his military campaign. His clever plan, in brief, was to drive a wedge between the south and the north and so prevent all the tribes joining in force against him. Once this had been accomplished he would overcome resistance in the south and then turn northwards to complete his task. The key to this operation was the strongly fortified city of Jericho which occupied a commanding position as the gateway to the west. If Jericho were destroyed, one of the greatest obstacles would be removed.

Two spies report on Jericho's defences

To test the strength of any future opposition, Joshua sent two spies from the camp at Shittim to Jericho. They secretly crossed the Jordan and were given shelter by a woman named Rahab in her house built on top of the city walls, as she knew quite well that the Israelites, so miraculously favoured by God, would conquer the city. The news that two strangers had been seen soon reached the king, who sent his officers ordering Rahab to surrender them. She had, however, hidden them amongst the stalks of flax on the roof after making them take an oath that she and her household would not perish when the city had fallen — a scarlet thread tied in the window would distinguish her house. Rahab told the officers that the two men had left the city at dusk, and they set out in hot pursuit. Rahab lowered the spies over the city wall and they hid for three days until the search was abandoned. They returned to Joshua and convinced him that the inhabitants of Jericho were terrified at the very thought of invasion by the Israelites.

The Israelites cross the river Jordan

The difficult task of transporting his army across the river Jordan now faced Joshua. On the tenth day of the first month (Nisan), with complete faith in the assurance given him by God, Joshua told the priests bearing the Ark of the Covenant to walk in front of the people, about a thousand yards ahead, so that the direction they followed could be easily seen. Fearlessly the priests stepped into the river and immediately the upper waters some distance away ceased to flow, and piled up into a heap. The lower waters continued their course towards the Dead Sea. The river bed therefore became dry, enabling everyone to pass over without difficulty. The priests advanced to the centre and remained there until everyone had crossed safely. Joshua gave orders for twelve stones to be set

45

up on the spot where the priests had stood, and for another twelve to be taken from the river bed to the other side. The priests then crossed the river and the waters resumed their normal course. The stones were erected as a memorial at Gilgal, in the plains of Jericho, which now became Joshua's military headquarters. After all the male Israelites had been circumcised, the Passover was observed on the evening of the fourteenth of Nisan, for the first time in the Holy Land. The manna, which had provided them with food during their wanderings in the wilderness (see page 26), ceased to fall.

Jericho is surrounded, and its walls collapse

Whilst Joshua was considering his next move, he suddenly saw an armed man holding a drawn sword. In reply to Joshua's challenge as to whether he was friend or foe, the man replied, 'I am captain of the Lord's host'. Joshua bowed down before him and was told to take his shoes off, for the place where he stood was holy. God directed Joshua how Jericho was to be captured, and he carried out the divine instructions.

Once a day, on six successive days, seven priests blowing a blast on rams' horns followed by priests carrying the Ark and armed forces moving silently at the rear, marched round the city walls. On the seventh day the circuit was made seven times, after which the trumpets gave out one long blast, the people

Outside the walls of Jericho

raised a mighty shout, and the city walls collapsed. Joshua uttered a solemn warning that the city, its inhabitants and cattle were to be utterly destroyed and no spoil kept for personal use; the gold and silver vessels of brass and iron were to be preserved for the holy Tabernacle. Each man rushed in

46

from the place where he stood and the city was destroyed by fire but Rahab and her household were conducted to safety by the two spies.

In recent years, excavations on the site of ancient Jericho have confirmed that a catastrophe overwhelmed the city and that its outer walls collapsed. Experts disagree as to the date, some suggesting 1400 B.C.E., and others 1200 B.C.E., but their discoveries certainly support the Biblical account of how Jericho fell.

The city of Ai is captured

To the north-west of Jericho stood the small city of Ai. Assured by his spies that it could easily be captured, Joshua sent about 3,000 soldiers to take it, but they were thrown back with the loss of thirty-six men. Joshua, in despair, consulted God, who revealed that the defeat was due to the theft of spoil taken in Jericho by one of his men. By casting lots, Achan, of the tribe of Judah, was discovered to be the offender. He confessed that he had hidden a valuable garment, silver and gold in his tent, and was put to death in the valley of Achor.

Joshua devised a clever plan to capture Ai. Dividing his troops into two battalions, he instructed one of them to lie in ambush behind the city while he, himself, led the other openly against the city. As he expected, the king of Ai led his army out of the city against Joshua who now pretended to flee and drew the inhabitants of Ai in hot pursuit. Joshua then raised his spear as a signal to the men in ambush who rushed into the city and set it on fire. Joshua turned against his pursuers so that they were caught between the two battalions and thoroughly defeated. This victory ensured a clear path for the victorious Israelites into the centre of Canaan.

A solemn ceremony is observed

Towards the end of his life, Moses had directed the people, once they had crossed the Jordan, to observe a solemn ceremony on Mounts Ebal and Gerizim. When Joshua reached Shechem, which lay in the valley between these two mountains, he carried out this instruction. On Mount Ebal, he built an altar of unhewn stones, and engraved on them a copy of the law of Moses. Then six tribes stood on Mount Gerizim to represent 'blessings', and six on Mount Ebal to represent 'curses'. The Levites, standing in the valley, pronounced curses on those who failed to obey twelve of the basic commandments, and corresponding blessings on those who obeyed them.

The remains of Joseph, which the Israelites had brought up with them out of Egypt (see page 24), were laid to rest in the city of Shechem.

The Gibeonites deceive Joshua

With the fall of Jericho and Ai, the Canaanite kings, realizing the danger, formed a league against the Israelites. The inhabitants of Gibeon, about six miles north-west of Jericho, terrified at the thought of being destroyed, sent a party of men to Gilgal, dressed in tattered garments and carrying with them stale provisions. They told Joshua that they had come from a distant land, had heard of the wonders performed by God, and asked for a covenant of peace with the Israelites. This was granted but the deception was soon discovered. Though eventually Joshua took command of Gibeon and its neighbouring three cities, he did not go back on his word. The Gibeonites, however, were forced to serve as hewers of wood and drawers of water.

Joshua comes to the aid of Gibeon

The five kings of the Amorites who lived in the south of Canaan, led by Adoni-Zedek, king of Jerusalem, determined to punish Gibeon for its act of treachery and besieged the city. Answering the call for help, Joshua and his men met the combined enemy forces and inflicted a heavy defeat on them. As they fled over the steep mountain passes of Beth-Horon leading to the valley of Ajalon, a violent storm broke out and the heavy hailstones killed even more than had fallen in combat. Night was about to fall, and Joshua was anxious to complete this military operation in daylight, so that none should escape under the cover of darkness. In his soldiers' presence, he called on the sun not to set, and on the moon not to rise. Miraculously, in the words of the Bible, 'the sun stood still, and the moon stayed, until the people had avenged themselves upon their enemies'.

In the meantime, the five kings had escaped to the south and hid in the cave of Makkedah where they were discovered. Joshua ordered the cave to be secured with rocks and guarded, and after the battle was over the kings were executed. This great victory against the Amorites was followed by the conquest of

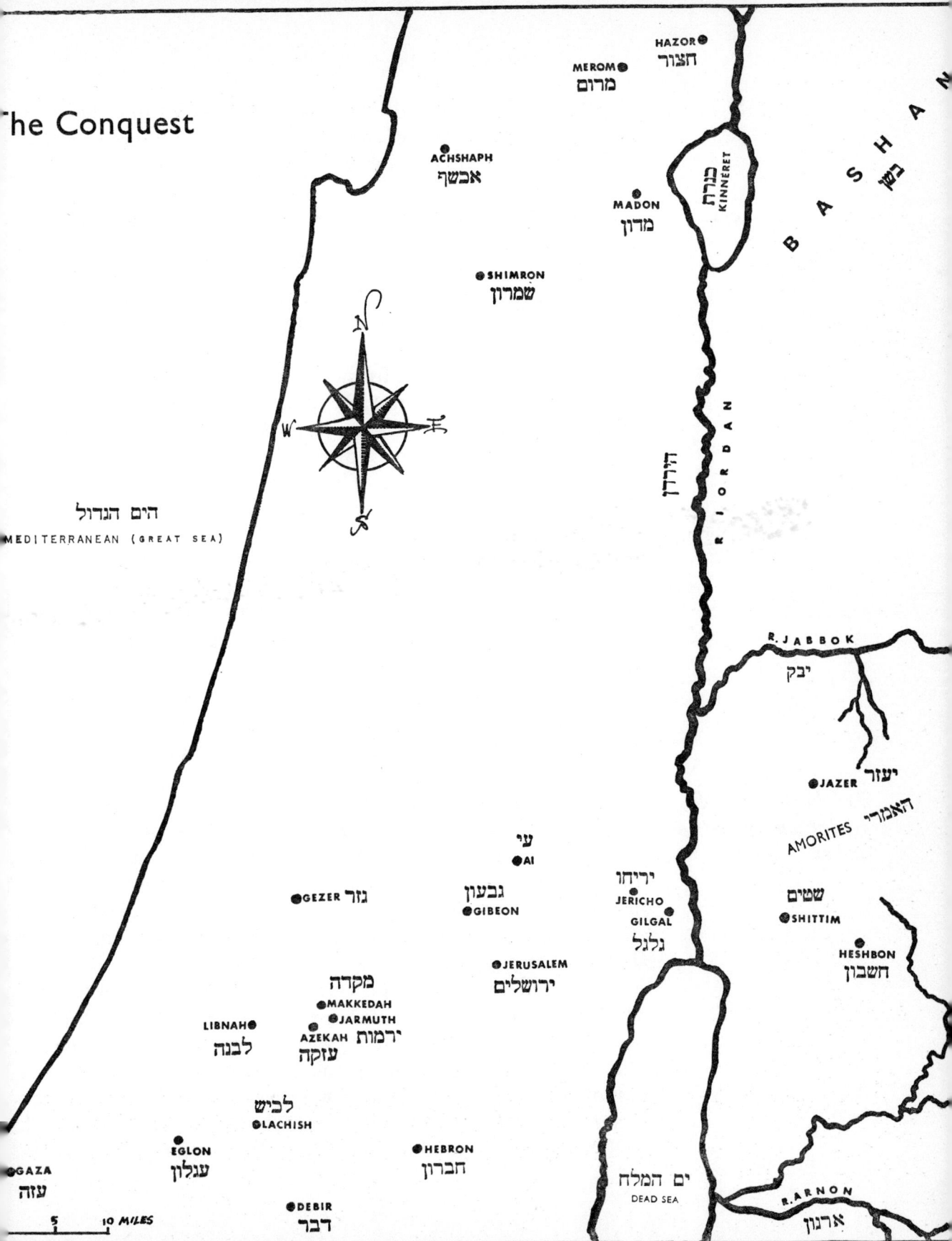

The Conquest

HAZOR חצור

MEROM מרום

ACHSHAPH אכשף

KINNÉRET כנרת

MADON מדון

SHIMRON שמרון

BASHAN בשן

R. JORDAN הירדן

R. JABBOK יבק

JAZER יעזר

AMORITES האמרי

הים הגדול
MEDITERRANEAN (GREAT SEA)

עי
AI

גבעון
GIBEON

GEZER גזר

ירחו
JERICHO

GILGAL גלגל

שטים
SHITTIM

JERUSALEM ירושלים

HESHBON חשבון

מקרה
MAKKEDAH
JARMUTH

LIBNAH
AZEKAH ירמות
עזקה

לבנה

לכיש
LACHISH

EGLON
עגלון

HEBRON חברון

GAZA
עזה

ים המלח
DEAD SEA

R. ARNON ארנון

DEBIR דבר

5   10 MILES

seven other kingdoms in the south, so that Joshua had now subdued most of the southern part of Canaan, and he returned to his headquarters at Gilgal.

Joshua conquers northern Canaan

In the north, the most important city was Hazor near the Sea of Galilee. Recent excavations on the site have shown that it was built on a large mound adjacent to a huge rectangular plateau. Altogether it occupied an area of about a hundred and seventy-five acres, providing accommodation for a population of forty thousand.

Jabin, king of Hazor, formed a league with all the kings of the north as far as Mount Hermon. They encamped near the waters of Merom, but in spite of their massive army and large numbers of chariots and horses, they proved no match for Joshua's lightning attack. The enemy fled in confusion and Joshua burnt the city of Hazor, 'the head of all these kingdoms', but left the others standing.

The war against the Canaanite tribes had lasted about seven years and altogether Joshua had defeated thirty-one kings and their cities on the west of the Jordan. This did not mean that every district and territory had been taken. Jerusalem, for instance, had not fallen, nor the plains along the Mediterranean which the Philistines inhabited, the coasts of Phoenicia and the mountain ranges of Lebanon. In fact, guerrilla warfare continued for many years long after Joshua had died.

The land is divided by lot among the tribes

Joshua was growing old and the time had come for the distribution of the land even though large regions were yet to be conquered. This difficult task was carried out by casting lots to decide the area to be occupied by each of the nine and a half tribes. (Reuben, Gad, and half the tribe of Manasseh had already received their allotment from Moses on the east of the Jordan, see page 42.)

At Gilgal, under the supervision of Joshua, Eleazar the High Priest, and the elders, territories were set aside for Judah, Ephraim and the other part of the tribe of Manasseh. Later, at Shiloh, where Joshua set up the Tabernacle, three men were appointed from each of the remaining seven tribes to conduct a survey of the rest of the land, which was then fairly divided.

The map on page 51 shows clearly the positions of the tribes.

Division of the Land

ZIDON צידון

ASHER אשר

NAPHTALI נפתלי

DAN דן

KEDESH קדש

MANASSEH מנשה

GOLAN גולן

ZEBULUN זבולן

ISSACHAR יששכר

RAMOTH GILEAD רמת גלעד

MANASSEH מנשה

SHECHEM שכם

GAD גד

DAN דן

EPHRAIM אפרים

BENJAMIN בנימין

BEZER בצר

REUBEN ראובן

JUDAH יהודה

HEBRON חברון

BEER SHEBA באר שבע

SIMEON שמעון

Mediterranean (Great Sea) הים הגדול

0   15   30
MILES

You will see that Judah received a large portion of land in the south. The tribe of Joseph does not appear but instead we find its two offshoots, Ephraim and Manasseh. Nor was land allotted to the tribe of Levi, but they did receive, for their maintenance, forty-eight cities with their suburbs on both sides of the Jordan (see page 42).

The division of the land completed, Joshua gave permission for the two and a half tribes to return to the east of Jordan.

Joshua's death

Before his death, Joshua addressed the leaders and reminded them of their glorious past. God had fulfilled his promise by giving them victory over the nations, and the people on their part must be loyal to His teachings and not mingle with the idolatrous inhabitants of Canaan or intermarry with them. 'Therefore be ye very courageous to keep and do all that is written in the book of the law of Moses.' At Shechem, Joshua reviewed Israel's past history and again emphasized the importance of obedience to God and His law.

Joshua died at the age of one hundred and ten and was buried in his own territory at Timnath-serah in the hill-country of Ephraim, near Shechem.

———————————>•⊂———————————

*Readings from
the Bible*

Joshua, chapter 1, verses 1 to 9   God's charge to Joshua
Joshua, chapter 3   Crossing of the Jordan
Joshua, chapter 6, verses 1 to 21   Fall of Jericho
Deuteronomy, chapter 27   Mounts Ebal and Gerizim
Joshua, chapter 24   Joshua's final address

Exercises

1. Draw an outline map and show by dotted lines the routes taken by Joshua in his various campaigns. Insert the more important towns and areas.
2. Give an account of Joshua's career *before* he succeeded Moses.
3. Can you suggest why Joshua was unable to conquer Jerusalem?
4. Write briefly on the following:
   (*a*) Rahab; (*b*) Achor; (*c*) the Gibeonites; (*d*) Jabin, king of Hazor.

9

IN THE DAYS OF THE JUDGES

*Local leaders, known
as 'judges', deliver
the people from
oppression*

AFTER Joshua's death, no outstanding leader emerged to unite all the people under one banner. Instead, each tribe had to protect itself, occasionally with the help of its neighbours, against constant assaults launched from both sides of the Jordan. In spite of Joshua's warning, many Israelites began to worship idols and to marry heathen women, with the disastrous result that they fell an easy prey to the enemy. This proved to be one of the darkest periods in history when 'there was no king in Israel, but every man did that which was right in his own eyes'. It lasted for a great many years until about the middle of the eleventh century B.C.E. In these troublesome days, there arose local leaders known as 'judges' who, through their bravery and inspiration, rescued their people from oppression. These leaders often acted as judges in the modern sense, giving decisions and interpreting the law. In this chapter, we shall be dealing with five of them.

In each case the pattern is the same. The Israelites worship idols, are oppressed, repent and are finally rescued. Ehud delivered them from the Moabites, Deborah from the northern Canaanites, Gideon from the Midianites, Jephthah from the Ammonites, and Samson from the Philistines.

*Ehud expels the
Moabites from
Benjamite territory*

Eglon, king of Moab, having formed an alliance with the Ammonites and Amalekites, crossed the Jordan and invaded the territory of Benjamin. He captured many important cities, and the people suffered under his oppression for eighteen years.

54

Their prayers for deliverance were answered by the appearance of Ehud, a Benjamite, who was chosen by his tribe to lead a delegation bringing a tribute to Eglon. After this had been presented, his companions withdrew but Ehud returned to the palace and requested an audience with the king, his excuse being that he wished to convey a private message. Normally, the king's visitors were searched in case they had concealed, on their left side, a weapon which they could quickly draw with their right hand. Ehud, however, was left-handed and he was able to hide his double-edged sword on his right side under his flowing robes without arousing suspicion.

Eglon agreed to receive Ehud in his summer parlour. Ehud approached him and said, 'I have a message from God for you' and, as the king rose from the couch on which he was reclining, Ehud drew his sword with his left hand and plunged it into Eglon's body. He then locked the door behind him, and by the time the servants discovered the king's corpse, was well on his way, eventually arriving at Mount Ephraim. There he rallied the Israelites, advanced towards the plain of Jericho, and occupied the fords of the Jordan to prevent the Moabites escaping across the river to their own country. Ehud's forces joined battle with the Moabites, whose army was completely annihilated — 'and the land had rest fourscore years'.

Charioteers

Deborah inspires Barak to defeat the northern Canaanites

We now turn to the north where Jabin, king of Hazor, like his ancestor of the same name, wielded great power. He possessed nine hundred iron chariots and the captain of his army was the mighty Sisera. For twenty years the northern Canaanites had oppressed the Israelites.

55

—RTDOO

In a house under a palm-tree between Ramah and Bethel in the hills of Ephraim lived the famous prophetess Deborah, whose wisdom as a judge was acknowledged by the whole nation, and the people turned to her for advice and help. She was determined to end their misery and sent a message to Barak, who lived in Kedesh-Naphtali, a city in the far north, to gather an army of ten thousand men from the tribes of Naphtali and Zebulun, and assemble them at Mount Tabor. There, she confidently predicted, Sisera's army would attack and be defeated. Barak asked Deborah to accompany him, for her inspiration was needed at this hour of crisis. She agreed, joined Barak at Kedesh where he mustered his troops, and they all went on to Mount Tabor. Meanwhile, Sisera's mighty army took up its position by the brook of Kishon, in the plain of Esdraelon.

Barak's men charged down from Mount Tabor's slopes and a fierce battle followed. There was no escape for Sisera's army in spite of their overwhelming numbers and iron chariots. Suddenly, a torrential storm burst over the plain. Sisera's soldiers panicked and their chariots became entangled in the marshy swamps. Realizing all was lost, Sisera fled to the tent of Jael, the wife of Heber the Kenite, who was friendly towards the Canaanites. Jael gave him shelter and food, and whilst he slept, exhausted by his recent experience, she killed him. She then waited for the pursuing Barak and led him into the tent where his enemy lay dead.

Deborah and Barak sang a song of thanksgiving in which they described how the Canaanites harassed Israel; how the call to unite against the common foe resulted in his defeat; and how Sisera was slain by Jael — 'and the land had rest forty years'.

Gideon is called to attack the Midianites

The next invaders were the Midianites and Amalekites who made frequent raids on Israeli territory, seizing crops, flocks and herds, and overran the country as far west as Gaza. The terrified Israelites abandoned their homes to live in dens, caves and strongholds. This oppression had lasted for seven years. In Ophrah, a city of Manasseh, lived Gideon, 'a mighty man of valour'. One day, whilst threshing wheat secretly in a winepress to hide it from the Midianites, he had a vision. An angel appeared and told him that he had been chosen by God to

56

deliver Israel. At first, Gideon was reluctant to undertake this mission, and asked for some sign to confirm the message. He ran into his house and brought out some meat, broth and unleavened cakes as an offering. The Divine messenger told Gideon to place them on a rock and, at the touch of his staff, fire consumed the offering, and the angel disappeared. Gideon was now ready to carry out God's commands, and his first move was to destroy the altar of Baal and other idolatrous shrines in his father's house. When this was discovered, the men of the city demanded Gideon's life but his father Joash replied, 'Let Baal contend for himself'. Gideon was afterwards also known as Jerubbaal, i.e., 'Let Baal contend'.

Gideon selects his army

The Midianites and Amalekites were encamped in the valley of Jezreel. Gideon gathered together an army of thirty-two thousand warriors from his own tribe and from those of Asher, Zebulun and Naphtali, and took up his position at En-harod, not far from the enemy. Gideon requested a further sign that Israel would be victorious. He spread a fleece of wool on his threshing floor, and asked that it be wet with dew while the earth around was dry. In the morning he wrung a bowlful of water from the fleece. At Gideon's renewed prayer, the same sign was reversed — the fleece was dry, whilst the earth around was wet with dew. Gideon was now fully convinced and to make sure that the coming victory would be ascribed to God's power he reduced the number of his men considerably. Twenty-two thousand men, who feared battle, were dismissed but there were still too many. Gideon took the remaining ten thousand down to a stream and watched them drink. The majority went down on their knees, but three hundred of them remained standing and lifted the water in their hands. By drinking in this way, they proved themselves reliable warriors always on the alert to meet a sudden attack.

The Midianites are defeated

That night Gideon and his armour bearer crept into the enemy camp and overheard one of the men relating a dream to his comrade. In this he had seen a cake of barley bread tumbling into the Midianite camp and overturning their captain's tent. His comrade interpreted the dream as meaning that Gideon would destroy the Midianite army.

Gideon then divided his small army of three hundred into three divisions, each man equipped with a trumpet and a pitcher containing a lighted torch. He advanced with his group and gave the signal by sounding his trumpet. All his soldiers blew their trumpets, broke their pitchers and waved their torches shouting the war-cry, 'The sword for the Lord and for Gideon'. The Midianites, bewildered by the tumult and blazing torches, were seized with panic, turned on each other and fled in confusion. They were prevented by the tribe of Ephraim from crossing the Jordan, and over a hundred and twenty thousand men and their chieftains were slain.

Gideon's exploits earned him national fame but he refused the offer to be crowned as king. 'The Lord shall rule over you' was his reply. He asked, however, for the golden ear-rings, captured as spoil, and from these he made a golden ephod (priestly garment) and set it up as a memorial in his home town of Ophrah. Unfortunately, the people revered it as though it were an idol, and, although there was peace for forty years, the people again worshipped Baal immediately after Gideon died.

Abimelech seizes the throne

One of Gideon's sons Abimelech, whose mother was a Canaanite woman of Shechem, coveted the throne. He gained support from the inhabitants of Shechem, and hired bandits to kill all his brothers, the only one to escape being Gideon's youngest son Jotham. Abimelech was proclaimed king at Shechem by the local citizens, but not by the entire nation. This election did not pass unchallenged. Jotham courageously ascended Mount Gerizim, overlooking Shechem, and told the people a parable. The trees, he said, wished to appoint a king over them and approached in turn the olive-tree, fig-tree and vine. But each refused, stating they were quite content to cultivate their own produce, which was beneficial to mankind. 'Then said all the trees unto the bramble: Come and reign over us. And the bramble said unto the trees: If in truth you anoint me king over you, then come and take refuge in my shadow; and if not, let fire come out of the bramble, and devour the cedars of Lebanon'.

In this way, Jotham warned them against the dangers of trusting in Abimelech whom he compared to the worthless bramble which, if set on fire, can do considerable damage.

58

Having delivered his message, Jotham fled into hiding. After Abimelech had reigned for three years, the people revolted and he retaliated by putting many of his former supporters to death. Whilst he was besieging the rebellious city of Thebez, a woman dropped a millstone from the roof of the city tower on Abimelech's head and crushed his skull. He implored his armourbearer to kill him rather than it should be said that he had perished by a woman's hand. So ended the short reign of an evil man.

Jephthah repels the Ammonites

Once again the Israelites were worshipping numerous idols. The punishment this time took the form of oppression by the Ammonites lasting eighteen years, especially in the land of Gilead on the east of the Jordan. The elders assembled at Mizpah and were prepared to wage war on their enemy, but a leader was lacking. A man named Jephthah was known to have the necessary qualities of leadership but had left his home-town in Gilead as his half-brothers refused to allow him to share in their father's inheritance. He had gone to live in the land of Tob, near the Syrian border, where he gathered around him a band of lawless men. The elders of Gilead now asked him to lead them in battle against the Ammonites. At first he refused but eventually accepted, provided they elected him as their chief — to which they agreed. Jephthah attempted by peaceful means to persuade the king of the Ammonites to withdraw. The king refused and Jephthah mustered his forces at Mizpah. Before setting out, he vowed that if he returned in peace, he would give up as a burnt offering 'whosoever should come forth of the doors of his house to meet him'. His expedition met with complete success and he captured twenty cities. On his return, to his horror, he was met by his only daughter. She accepted her fate, requesting only that for two months she live quietly on the mountains. Jephthah judged Israel for six years.

Samson takes revenge on the Philistines

The Philistines, it is thought, originally came from Crete and eventually settled on the south-west maritime plain of Canaan where they became very powerful and built many strong cities. For forty years they harassed the Israelites, especially the neighbouring tribe of Dan. In accordance with a promise made in a vision to a man named Manoah and his wife, who lived in

59

the small city of Zorah, a son named Samson was born to them who, they were told, would deliver Israel from the Philistines. He was brought up as a Nazarite, which meant that he never took strong drink and his hair was never cut. As he grew to manhood, he was endowed with superhuman strength and great courage. Samson moved freely among the enemy and displeased his parents by wishing to marry a Philistine woman. The Bible records a number of his adventures — here are four of them:

Samson's riddle

(i) On his way to Timnah to visit his intended Philistine bride, he tore apart with his bare hands a young lion which rushed out upon him. When he passed that way again he saw that a swarm of bees had built their hive in the lion's carcass and he ate some of the honey. At the wedding feast, he put a riddle to thirty of his Philistine companions, to be solved within seven days, the stake being thirty changes of apparel. The riddle was, 'Out of the eater came forth food, and out of the strong came forth sweetness'. The men, unable to find the answer, threatened Samson's wife and her family with death unless she persuaded her husband to disclose it to her. On the seventh day, they were able to reply, 'What is sweeter than honey? And what is stronger than a lion?' Samson, guessing that his wife had given the answer, killed thirty Philistines in Ashkelon and gave their garments to his companions who had solved the riddle. He then left his bride and returned to his father's house in Zorah.

The burning of the crops

(ii) Some time later, Samson wished to be reconciled with his wife only to find that her father, thinking Samson hated her, had given her to another. Samson, in rage, took three hundred foxes, tied them tail to tail, with a lighted firebrand between each pair, and let them loose in the Philistines' cornfields, vineyards and olive-yards. This caused immense damage, and the Philistines blamed Samson's wife and her father for their misfortunes and put them to death. Samson took revenge by killing a large number of Philistines.

A feat of strength

(iii) The Philistines marched against Judah and demanded Samson's surrender. Bound with two strong cords, Samson was

60

brought down to the Philistine camp and was received with a shout of triumph. But Samson broke the cords and, seizing the jawbone of an ass, killed a thousand Philistines.

Escape from Gaza

(iv) Whilst he was staying in Gaza, his enemies closed the gates of the city intending to kill him in the morning, but at midnight Samson unhinged the two huge gates and carried them on his shoulders to the top of a hill near Hebron. This and similar exploits made him famous as a man of outstanding courage and he became the acknowledged champion of the Israelites for twenty years.

Samson's heroic death

Samson fell in love with Delilah, a Philistine woman, who was bribed by the chieftains to try and find out wherein lay Samson's strength. After she had made several unsuccessful attempts, he revealed the secret that his strength lay in his hair. Whilst he was sound asleep, Delilah ordered his hair to be cut off, and the Philistines seized him, blinded him and bound him in chains. They put him in prison where he was made to grind corn, but as Samson's hair grew again his strength returned.

A festive celebration was being held in the temple of Dagon, and Samson was sent for so that the Philistines could make fun of him. After Samson had performed some feats of strength for them he asked his guide to let him lean on the two main pillars which supported the temple roof. He prayed to God for strength, pushed the pillars apart, and the whole building collapsed in ruins, killing all those who were assembled. Samson's relatives rescued his body and buried him in the family burial place in the territory of Dan.

The Danites realized they could not continue to live near the Philistines, and decided to seek a new home. They eventually settled in the extreme north, where they conquered the city of Laish and renamed it Dan.

The story of Ruth

During the dangerous days of the judges, the Bible records a peaceful episode about the private lives of two women, Naomi and Ruth. Elimelech, his wife Naomi, and his two sons, Mahlon and Chilion, left Bethlehem in Judah because of famine, and stayed in the country of Moab. Elimelech died and his sons married Moabite women, Orpah and Ruth. After a few years, the two sons died and Naomi, hearing the famine had ended, decided to return to Bethlehem. Orpah remained behind but Ruth insisted on accompanying her mother-in-law — 'Whither thou goest, I will go . . . thy people shall be my people, and thy God my God'.

They reached Bethlehem at the beginning of the barley harvest. Naomi sent Ruth to the field of Boaz, a close relative of Elimelech, and she was allowed special privileges when gleaning among the sheaves of corn. Boaz was ready to accept the responsibility — which fell upon near relatives — for re-purchasing the land formerly owned by Elimelech and keeping it within the family. He also wished to marry Ruth so that their heir would inherit the property. A closer relative, however, had a prior right to perform the duty but was unwilling to accept it. Soon after, Boaz married Ruth and they had a son named Obed who became the grandfather of David, the future king of Israel.

Readings from the Bible

Judges, chapter 4, verses 4 to 24	The story of Deborah
Judges, chapter 6, verses 11 to 32	Call of Gideon
Judges, chapter 9, verses 7 to 21	Jotham's Parable
Judges, chapter 14, verses 12 to 20	Samson's riddle
Judges, chapter 16, verses 4 to 22	The story of Delilah
Ruth, chapter 1	Ruth's loyalty

Exercises

1. Indicate, on a map, the areas occupied by the enemies who attacked Israel during the period of the Judges.
2. When is the song of Deborah read in the Synagogue, and why?
3. Make a list of the judges mentioned in this chapter, and explain, in each case, why he or she rose to such prominence.
4. Which Jewish festival do you connect with the Book of Ruth? Give the reasons for your answer.

10

RISE OF THE MONARCHY

Samuel receives
a call from God

AFTER the death of Samson, the powerful Philistines began a military campaign against the Israelites. One of the main objects of their attack was the city of Shiloh, the religious centre of the whole country, in which the Tabernacle had stood since the days of Joshua (see page 52). The aged Eli, a descendant of Ithamar, Aaron's youngest son, had ministered there as High Priest and judge for forty years. He was highly respected but had no influence over his dishonest sons, Hophni and Phinehas, who forcibly took more than their due share of the people's offerings. Under Eli's care was a young lad named Samuel, who had been dedicated to God's service by his mother Hannah.

Hannah, the wife of Elkanah, a Levite, had been childless. On one of their annual visits to Shiloh from Ramah, where they lived, she prayed for a child, and vowed that if it were a son she would dedicate him to God's service. Though her lips moved she uttered no sound. Eli thought she was drunk, but when he heard of her sorrow, expressed the hope that God would grant her petition. In due course Samuel was born and, as soon as he was weaned, Hannah left him in Eli's charge. Elkanah and his family came up yearly to Shiloh to offer a sacrifice and on each occasion Hannah brought a gift of a new coat for her small son.

One night, the young Samuel was aroused from his sleep by a voice calling him by name. He ran to Eli, thinking he had been summoned, but was told he was mistaken. This happened a second time. On the third occasion, Eli realized Samuel was

63

being called by God, and told him to return to his bed and answer, 'Speak, Lord, for Thy servant heareth'. Samuel did so, and heard God's voice telling him that Eli's family was doomed because of his sons' wickedness. On Eli's insistence, Samuel repeated the message and the old priest, who had already received a similar warning from one of the prophets, humbly accepted God's decision. From that day onwards, Samuel received Divine revelations, and was soon recognized by all Israel as a prophet of the Lord.

The Ark is captured by the Philistines, but later returned

A decisive battle between the Philistines and Israelites was fought near Aphek, where the Israelites were defeated with a loss of about four thousand men. They regrouped their army at their camp in Eben-ezer and decided to renew the attack, supported by the presence of the holy Ark, which, they thought, would turn the tide in their favour. The arrival of the Ark, brought by Hophni and Phinehas, was the signal for great jubilation. The Philistines, in spite of their fear at this new danger, fought courageously, and won an overwhelming victory. Not only did they kill thirty thousand men, including Eli's two sons, but they also captured the Ark. Eli, who was ninety-eight years of age, collapsed when he heard the dreadful news, and died.

Excavations in this region confirm the destruction of a number of cities, including Shiloh, about the year 1050 B.C.E. It can be assumed, therefore, that the Philistines followed up their victory at Aphek by an advance towards the east.

Triumphantly, the Philistines carried the Ark to Ashdod, one of their chief cities, and placed it in the temple of their god Dagon. On two successive mornings, they found their idol lying on its face before the Ark, the second time broken in pieces. At the same time, the people of Ashdod were afflicted with a painful disease. They refused to keep the Ark any longer and sent it to Gath, a neighbouring city. There, too, the epidemic spread amongst the inhabitants, and the Ark was sent on to Ekron, but the Ekronites refused to keep it in their city. The Ark remained in enemy hands for seven months, and at last the Philistines decided to send it back to Israel. They put it on a cart, drawn by two cows, and sent it on its way. The cows took the straight route into Israelite territory and came to a halt at Beth-shemesh. The resultant rejoicing was short-

64

lived, for the citizens of Beth-shemesh, overcome by curiosity, opened the Ark and looked into it. This act of irreverence was punished by the outbreak of a plague, and the Ark eventually rested in the house of Abinadab in Kiryath-jearim, where it remained until David removed it to Jerusalem (see page 83).

Samuel's inspiring leadership unites the people

For the next twenty years the Israelites were forced to submit to Philistine domination. Although they went on with their normal duties, they dared not assemble in large numbers for fear of an attack by their oppressors. During this period, Samuel did everything possible to keep the spark of religious and national feeling alive among his people. He lived in Ramah, his home town, but went once a year on circuit to Bethel, Gilgal and Mizpah to judge and instruct the people. He also founded 'schools of the prophets' at which selected men were trained to act as religious leaders.

Samuel felt that the moment had arrived when he could re-unite Israel as a people consecrated to God's service, and called upon them to abandon the Baalim and Ashtaroth (the male and female Canaanite deities) which they had worshipped. They immediately complied with his request and this encouraged Samuel to summon the nation to Mizpah for a day of prayer and supplication. The Philistines, hearing of this assembly, mustered their troops and marched towards the city. The prophet prayed for Divine aid. As the enemy approached, a violent thunderstorm burst over their heads and, seized with panic, they fled in all directions. The Israelites gained a complete victory, and recaptured all the cities they had formerly lost. Many years elapsed before the Philistines dared venture forth again from the narrow coastal strip to which they were confined.

The people demand a king

Although the country was at peace, there was great uneasiness about the future. The prophet was growing old, and his two sons, Joel and Abijah, whom he had appointed as assistant judges in Beersheba, proved unworthy of their father, for they accepted bribes and gave false verdicts. Furthermore, the Israelites wished to be like other nations and have a permanent warrior to lead them in battle. For these reasons the elders visited Samuel at Ramah, and demanded the election of a king. Samuel was naturally hurt at the thought that the people no longer had confidence in him. Nevertheless, he prayed for Divine guidance and was told to agree to their request but to warn them that a king would assume dictatorial powers, force them into military and domestic service, impose heavy taxes and take possession of their lands. This had no effect, and the people persisted in their demands.

Saul is anointed and proclaimed as king

The man selected to be the first king of Israel was Saul, the son of Kish, a Benjamite, who lived in Gibeah. His father's asses had strayed and Saul, accompanied by a servant, was sent to find them. They searched high and low without success, and as Saul was about to return home, his servant suggested they consult the seer at Ramah. Samuel had received a Divine communication to expect Saul's arrival and to anoint him as king. The prophet met Saul and invited him to a feast to be held in celebration of a communal sacrifice to be offered that day, and assured him that the asses had been found. He then startled Saul by continuing, 'On whom is all the desire of Israel? Is it not on you, and on all your father's house?' Taken aback, Saul answered, 'Am I not a Benjamite, of the smallest of the tribes of Israel? Wherefore then do you speak so to me?' After the meal, Saul stayed the night at Samuel's house. The next morning at the city gate, and in strict privacy, Samuel poured oil on Saul's head and told him that God had anointed him to be a prince over His inheritance.

To convince Saul that he was God's choice, the prophet foretold three events which would occur as he returned home: (i) two men would meet him near Rachel's tomb and tell him that his father's asses had been found; (ii) at the oak of Tabor, he would be presented with two loaves of bread by three men taking offerings to the sanctuary of Bethel; and (iii) at Gibeah, he would meet a company of prophets carrying musical instruments. Saul, too, would be moved by the spirit of God and prophesy with them. All these signs were fulfilled, and when the people saw Saul prophesying, they asked with astonishment, 'What is this that is come unto the son of Kish? Is Saul also among the prophets?' On his return home, Saul did not talk about the secret conversations between him and Samuel.

Shortly afterwards, Samuel convened a general assembly at Mizpah, and proceeded to elect a king by casting lots. The

66

choice fell on Saul who had modestly hidden himself. When he was brought before his subjects, they were greatly impressed by his imposing stature and appearance, 'for he was higher than any of the people from his shoulders and upward'. And all Israel shouted in admiration, 'Long live the king'. Only a minority expressed doubts as to his capabilities but they were soon to be proved mistaken.

Saul comes to the rescue of Jabesh-gilead

Saul commenced his reign about the year 1025 B.C.E. Before he could be certain of the wholehearted support of his people, he had to prove his worth as a military leader. The opportunity soon presented itself when Nahash, king of the Ammonites, besieged Jabesh-gilead, an Israelite city on the east side of the Jordan. Its inhabitants were willing to surrender but Nahash laid down the condition that they must each submit to the loss of the right eye, which meant they would never be able to fight again. The elders of the city asked for a week's respite and sent an appeal for help to Gibeah, Saul's home town. Saul was ploughing the fields when he heard of this demand. He cut two of his oxen in pieces and sent them to all the tribes, threatening that this would be the fate of all their cattle if they did not rally round his banner. A huge army of 330,000 men responded to his call, and he swiftly fell upon the Ammonites, defeating them with enormous losses. This striking victory firmly established Saul's reputation as a man of courage and determination.

The confirmation of Saul as king took place at Gilgal with great rejoicing. Samuel was now ready to hand over his authority to the new ruler. In a stirring address, he called upon the Israelites to bear witness to his integrity as a judge and reminded them of their glorious history; if they remained true to God they would never be forsaken.

The Philistines launch an attack

The Philistines had, once again, taken over a number of important cities in the territory occupied by the tribe of Benjamin, and now constituted a real danger to Saul. His army consisted of three thousand selected men, a third of whom were under the command of his eldest son, Jonathan, at Gibeah. Saul himself was stationed at Michmas with the remaining troops. Jonathan struck the first blow against the enemy by wiping out the Philistine garrison at Geba (a few miles north-east of Gibeah), which faced Michmas across a deep ravine. The Philistines promptly replied to the challenge by assembling a huge army, and captured the town of Michmas. Saul was forced to retreat to Gilgal. The terrified Israelites took refuge in caves and rocks, and some even crossed the Jordan to find shelter in the land of Gilead.

Saul disobeys
Samuel

Saul was no coward, and with his depleted army of only six hundred men made preparations at Gilgal for a counter-attack. He waited impatiently for Samuel who had promised to come in seven days' time to offer up sacrifices before the battle was resumed. On the seventh day, as the prophet had not yet arrived, Saul grew restless and offered the sacrifices himself. At this moment Samuel arrived and denounced the king for his disobedience and lack of faith. The first duty of a king was to obey the prophet who spoke in God's name. Saul was told that his kingdom would not continue for 'the Lord has sought out a man after His own heart . . . to be prince over His people'.

Jonathan surprises
the enemy

Saul and his small army joined Jonathan at the garrison of Geba, waiting hopelessly for a change in his fortunes. It was Jonathan's bravery which decided the outcome of this long and protracted war. One day, without his father's knowledge, and accompanied by his armour-bearer, the young prince climbed down into the ravine that separated Geba from Michmas. They then secretly ascended the steep cliff on the opposite side and Jonathan decided to show himself to the Philistines who were guarding one of the advanced posts. Jeeringly the sentries called out, 'Come up to us, and we will show you a thing'. This was the omen for which Jonathan was waiting. He scrambled up the precipice and, with his armour-bearer, killed twenty of the astonished soldiers. The Philistines quickly discovered that their stronghold was captured and thought that a massive army was moving against them. The resulting panic, increased by a sudden earthquake, made the enemy flee in all directions.

From his camp, Saul saw the enemy in flight and immediately followed in pursuit. He was joined by the men who had gone into hiding, and the Philistines were driven back. In the heat of the moment Saul had threatened with the death penalty anyone who tasted food before nightfall until the enemy was finally defeated. Jonathan, ignorant of his father's command, refreshed himself with some honey he had found in the forest. When Saul heard that his son had disobeyed his order he was quite ready to carry out his threat. Only the intervention of the people, who hailed Jonathan as a conqueror, prevented such a tragedy.

Saul disobeys the command to destroy the Amalekites

Saul followed up his success with a series of victories over all his enemies on every side, the Moabites and Ammonites in the east, the Edomites in the south, and the Syrian kingdom of Zobah in the north. There still remained the Amalekites, the nomad race in the Negeb. Samuel reminded Saul of their treachery in the past (see page 26) and told him, in God's name, to destroy them and their possessions utterly. Saul, with his massive army of 210,000 men, had little difficulty in achieving success but spared Agag, the Amalekite king, and saved the best of the captured sheep and cattle for sacrifice to God. Saul returned to Gilgal, and it was again Samuel's sad duty to rebuke the king for disobeying God's command — 'Because thou hast rejected the word of the Lord, He has also rejected thee from being king'. In response to Saul's earnest plea not to put him to shame before the people, the prophet remained whilst the king prayed to God for forgiveness. Samuel then sent for Agag and executed him. The king and prophet parted company and were never to see each other again.

Readings from the Bible

I Samuel, chapter 1, verses 1 to 18   Hannah prays for a child
I Samuel, chapter 3   Call of Samuel
I Samuel, chapter 8   The people demand a king
I Samuel, chapter 15, verses 10 to 23   Samuel rebukes Saul

Exercises

1. Draw an outline map, and show the areas and more important towns where the battles with the Philistines took place.
2. Why was Samuel so reluctant to meet the people's demands for a king? (Before replying, read Deuteronomy, chapter 17, verses 14 to 19.)
3. Describe an incident illustrating the bravery of (*a*) Saul and (*b*) Jonathan.
4. Who said the following, and under what circumstances?
   (*a*) Am I not better to thee than ten sons?
   (*b*) Make us a king to judge us like all the nations.
   (*c*) Cursed be the man that eateth any food until it be evening.
   (*d*) Behold, to obey is better than sacrifice.

11

SAUL AND DAVID

David is anointed as Saul's successor

SAMUEL was next commissioned by God to go to Jesse — a grandson of Ruth the Moabitess — who lived in Bethlehem in Judah, and anoint one of his sons as successor to the throne. To avoid making Saul suspicious, the prophet was to tell the inhabitants that he had come to offer a sacrifice. Samuel invited Jesse and his sons to attend the feast which followed. On seeing the handsome and tall Eliab, the eldest, the prophet felt convinced that this was the chosen one. But he heard God's voice telling him not to be misled by outward appearances, 'for the Lord looks on the heart'. Seven of Jesse's sons passed in succession before Samuel, without his receiving any sign. When he inquired if any remained, Jesse sent for David, his youngest, who was away at the time tending his father's flocks. David was a fine-looking youth with a pleasant personality, who had already gained a reputation as a gifted poet and musician. He had also shown great courage in protecting the flocks from attacks by wild animals. Samuel received the Divine communication for which he had waited: 'Arise, anoint him; for this is he.' The ceremony was performed in private; only his brothers were there. It was essential that Saul should not get to know what had happened.

Meanwhile Saul was becoming more and more depressed. His final encounter with Samuel had made it clear beyond doubt that his son Jonathan, would not succeed him, and he was often seized with fits of melancholy. His advisers suggested he employ a skilled player on the harp to soothe him when the occasion arose. One of the courtiers recommended David, not

70

only as a musician but also as a man of valour and prudence. In this way David became Saul's personal attendant and armour-bearer.

David accepts Goliath's challenge

Some years had elapsed since the battle of Michmas (see page 68), and the Philistines felt strong enough to return to the attack. They encamped at Ephes-dammim, on the frontier hills of Judah, whilst the Israelites, separated from their foes by a deep ravine, occupied the mountain range overlooking the vale of Elah. Neither side was willing to make the first move and so put itself in danger. The Philistines had among them a champion of Gath named Goliath, who was over nine feet tall. Morning and evening, for forty days, this giant came out and challenged the Israelites to choose a man to fight him, and proposed that the nation whose champion was defeated should surrender.

David happened to arrive at the very moment when Goliath was making his usual challenge, for Jesse had sent his youngest son to the camp with provisions for his three elder brothers who were serving in Saul's army. David expressed contempt for the Philistine, and the bystanders told him that the king had offered great riches and his daughter's hand in marriage to the man who killed Goliath. Saul was informed of David's bold defiance and sent for him, but expressed doubts as to his ability to accept the challenge, as he was only a youth. David then told the king how, single-handed, he had killed a bear and a lion which attacked his sheep, and expressed his confidence in God's help. The king finally agreed to allow him to make the attempt.

David had to remove the heavy armour supplied by the king as it hampered his movements. Armed with nothing but his staff, five smooth stones and a sling, he approached Goliath, who shouted contemptuously, 'Am I a dog, that you come to me with staves?' But David confidently aimed one of his stones with such force and accuracy that it pierced the Philistine's forehead and he fell to the ground. David ran forward and, drawing Goliath's sword from its sheath, cut off the giant's head. When the Philistines saw their champion was dead, they fled, and the Israelites pursued them as far as Gaza and Ekron. David retained Goliath's armour as a trophy.

David's victory over Goliath established his reputation as a warrior, and Saul appointed him as one of his captains. His greatest admirer was Jonathan, Saul's eldest son, who presented him with his armour and sword, and became David's closest friend. Then an incident occurred which completely changed Saul's attitude towards David. When the soldiers returned to Gibeah after their victory, the women came out to meet them, and as they played their instruments they sang, 'Saul hath slain his thousands, but David his ten thousands'. This was enough to arouse suspicions in Saul's mind that David might well be the rival to the throne of whom Samuel had spoken. Next day, in one of his fits of gloom, he threw his javelin at David as he played his harp, but David fortunately managed to escape injury.

David kills Goliath

The king was haunted by a jealous fear, and began to plot against David's life. He promised him the hand of his eldest daughter, Merab, provided he gained more military successes. David returned safely from all his expeditions but Merab was given in marriage to another man. David does not seem to have been disappointed for Michal, Saul's youngest daughter, had fallen in love with him. The king gave his consent to their marriage on condition that David killed one hundred Philistines, hoping he would fall in battle. David returned safely after killing two hundred of the enemy, and the king had no alternative but to fulfil his promise.

*David's life is
endangered*

Saul's evil temper increased to such an extent that he even tried to persuade Jonathan to kill David. Jonathan, however, argued with his father, reminding him of David's services to

72

his people, and Saul, in one of his calmer moods, promised that David would not be put to death. David returned to the court, but when he made yet another successful attack on the enemy, Saul, in a fit of fury, again threw a javelin at him. David was now really frightened, and hurried home. Saul sent his men to surround the house and wait for an opportunity to kill David, but Michal helped her husband escape during the night by letting him down through the window.

David takes refuge with Samuel

David made his way to Ramah, told Samuel what had happened, and stayed with him at Naioth, where the school of prophets was housed. Saul soon learned of David's whereabouts, and sent his messengers to arrest him, but, when they saw the prophets prophesying, they were overcome by religious ecstasy and also prophesied. A second and third band of messengers followed in succession, and on each occasion were similarly affected. Finally Saul himself came to Naioth but he, too, could not resist the prophetic urge. This incident gave new force to the proverb, 'Is Saul also among the prophets?' (see page 66).

Jonathan warns David

David met Jonathan secretly and they agreed to make one final effort to find out what Saul meant to do. At the feast held in celebration of the New Moon, instead of appearing as usual at the king's table, David hid himself in a nearby field. Saul noticed David's absence but passed no comment. On the second day he asked Jonathan the reason. Jonathan replied that he had permitted David to attend a family feast at Bethlehem. Saul was very angry and, after taunting his son for befriending David, hurled his javelin at him. On the following morning Jonathan went into the field and shot three arrows towards a target. As his young attendant ran to pick them up, Jonathan called out, 'Is not the arrow beyond thee?' This was the pre-arranged signal to indicate that the king was determined to put David to death. When the lad had left the field, the friends embraced and swore everlasting friendship. Jonathan returned home whilst David went into voluntary exile.

Saul's hatred became so intense that he married off his daughter Michal, David's wife, to another man.

David's adventures in exile	Until Saul's death, David was constantly on the run, seeking shelter even in enemy territory. During this period, he composed a number of psalms in which he expressed his trust in God who delivered him from his enemies. In spite of Saul's hatred, never once did he make any attempt on the king's life, for he had complete confidence that God was guiding his destiny.

We shall now deal briefly with David's adventures as a fugitive from Saul:

The city of Nob

(i) David came to Nob, a small city near Jerusalem, where the Tabernacle had been transferred after the fall of Shiloh. Ahimelech, the priest, was surprised to see him without his usual retinue, but David, not wishing to involve the saintly man, told him he was on a private mission for the king. He asked for food and was given some sacred loaves of showbread, and also obtained Goliath's sword which had been preserved in the sanctuary. Unfortunately, Doeg, the Edomite, who was the king's chief herdsman, was present at the time and later reported the incident to Saul. The king immediately sent for Ahimelech and all the priests of Nob and accused them of conspiracy. He sentenced them to death but none of his guards would carry out his cruel order. Doeg alone obeyed the king's command and killed eighty-five priests. The inhabitants of the city of Nob were massacred, the only one to escape being Abiathar, Ahimelech's son, who joined David in exile, bringing with him the priestly ephod.

Gath

(ii) From Nob, David made his way to the court of Achish, king of Gath, but the Philistines soon recalled his former hostility, and he saved his life only by pretending to be mad and was sent away.

The cave of Adullam

(iii) In one of the caves of Adullam, near Bethlehem, where David took refuge for a time, he was joined by his family and by about four hundred rebels and adventurers. Anxious about his parents' safety he placed them in the care of the king of Moab, who was hostile towards Saul for having invaded his territory (see page 69).

Keilah and the wilderness of Ziph

(iv) Although David delivered the city of Keilah, some three miles south of Adullam, from Philistine raids, its ungrateful inhabitants were quite prepared to surrender him to Saul. David therefore fled to the wilderness of Ziph where Jonathan met him, in secret, for the last time. The prince assured his lifelong friend that Saul would never find him and that he would be king of Israel. The Ziphites betrayed David's movements to Saul, so he went further south to the wilderness of Maon. Saul was on the point of closing in on David, when he was suddenly called away to repel a Philistine invasion.

Engedi

(v) David was hiding at Engedi, on the western shore of the Dead Sea, when he was once again hunted by Saul, who had returned from battle. By chance, Saul rested in the very cave where David and his men were concealed. His followers urged him to kill Saul, but David refused to raise his hand against the Lord's anointed and contented himself by cutting off a corner of Saul's royal robe. When Saul awoke, David followed him out of the cave and produced the corner of his robe to show that he had spared the king's life. Saul was deeply moved, acknowledged David's generosity and implored him to spare his family when he came to the throne. David remained in the stronghold of Engedi, for past experience had taught him not to rely on Saul's promises.

About this time Samuel died and was mourned by all Israel. He was buried in the grounds of his own house at Ramah.

The story of Nabal

(vi) At this stage an interesting episode occurred which illustrates how David and his outlaws protected people's property in return for food. On the mountain-range of Carmel dwelt a rich sheep-owner named Nabal, whose flock had been protected from raiders by David's men. When Nabal was shearing his sheep, David sent some of his men requesting a gift. He replied insultingly, 'Who is David? . . . There are many servants nowadays who break away every man from his master'. David resolved to avenge the insult but fortunately Nabal's wife, the gentle and prudent Abigail, went to meet him and his men, bringing with her a plentiful supply of provisions. In courteous language she frankly admitted Nabal's folly, and pleaded with David not to shed blood. David responded favourably to her plea and blessed her for her intervention. The following day Abigail told her husband of his lucky escape and he was seized with a stroke, from which he died. Soon after David married Abigail.

Return to the wilderness of Ziph

(vii) David returned to his former hiding-place in the wilderness of Ziph, where he was again sought out by Saul. In the dead of night, accompanied only by his nephew Abishai, David penetrated through the lines to the place where both the king and Abner, his commander-in-chief, lay asleep. Abishai asked permission to kill Saul, but David refused and contented himself with taking away the king's spear and cruse of water.

David's Wanderings

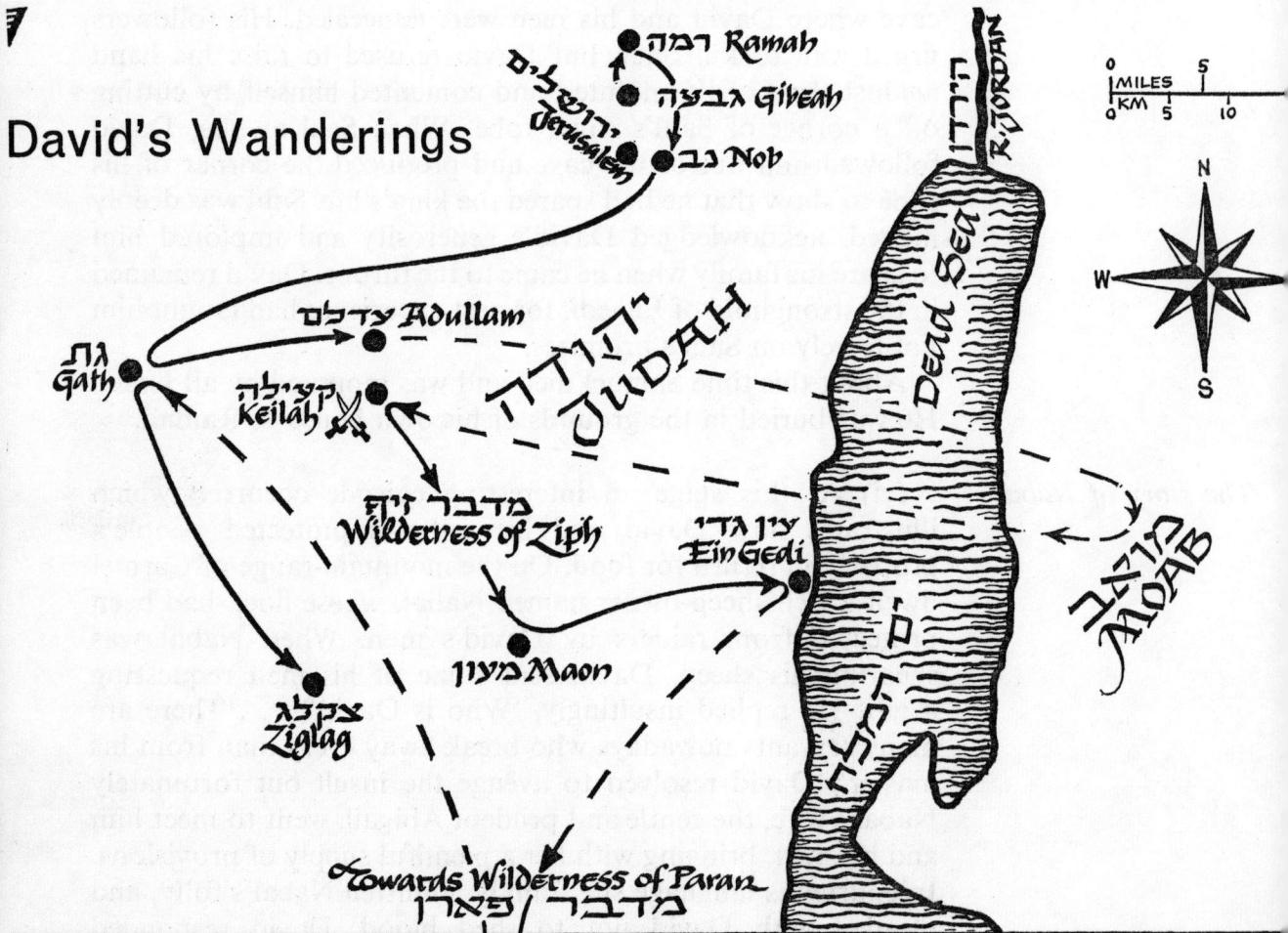

David then climbed to the top of a neighbouring hill and called out to Abner, taunting him for not protecting the king properly. Saul recognized David's voice and again acknowledged his guilt — 'I have played the fool and erred exceedingly'.

Return to Gath

(viii) Saul returned to Gibeah but David, recognizing that his position was desperate, decided to seek refuge once again with the king of Gath. This time he brought with him his band of men, now increased to six hundred. Achish welcomed him as a true ally in their common struggle against Saul, and gave him the city of Ziklag as a residence. From there he made several raids on nomadic tribes but pretended to Achish that he was fighting the Israelites in the Negeb. When Saul heard that David had settled in Philistine territory, he decided to call off any further attempts to capture him.

Achish sends David back to Ziklag

Preparations were being made by the Philistines for another contest with the Israelites, and Achish summoned David and his followers to accompany him to Aphek, where the united Philistine forces had gathered. David found himself in a dilemma, for he could not fight his own people. Fortunately for him, the military commanders were suspicious of his loyalty and Achish instructed David to leave Aphek and return to Ziklag. On arriving there, he discovered that during his absence the Amalekites had plundered the city and carried off his wives. David lost no time in pursuing them. The enemy was overtaken and only four hundred young men escaped death by riding away on their swift camels. David rescued his wives, brought back much spoil, and sent gifts to the elders of Judah and to various cities whose inhabitants had befriended him during his exile.

Saul consults the witch of Endor

By this time the massive Philistine army had advanced to the valley of Jezreel, in the heart of northern Israel. They occupied the slopes near Shunem while Saul and the Israelites were encamped on the opposite hills of Gilboa. The gloomy and despondent Saul was seized with fear at the sight of the Philistine army. He had no prophet or priest to turn to for advice and, in despair, went to consult a woman who lived in Endor and who claimed she could conjure up the spirits of the dead.

Saul went to her at night and in disguise, and asked her to bring up from the dead the person he would name. The woman feared a trap, for a royal decree had forbidden any form of witchcraft. Saul took an oath she would not be punished and told her to bring up Samuel. The witch exercised her art and claimed to see 'an old man coming up, covered with a robe'. In his delirium, Saul assumed it was Samuel and asked for his advice. The spirit replied it was useless to consult him for God had given the kingdom to David. 'Tomorrow', said the voice, 'shalt thou and thy sons be with me'. At this sentence, Saul fainted with fear and exhaustion. He slowly recovered after eating a hastily prepared meal and returned to the camp the same night.

Saul and Jonathan die in the battle of Gilboa

The next day the Philistines launched a fierce attack which extended over the mountain ranges of Gilboa. The Israelites were defeated with heavy losses and among those killed were three of the king's sons, including the valiant Jonathan. Saul was severely wounded by an arrow and begged his armour-bearer to thrust him through with his sword. On his refusal, Saul fell upon his own sword and died, and his faithful attendant followed his example and killed himself. When the Philistines came to strip the slain they found the bodies of Saul and his sons and hanged them on the wall of Beth-shan. The citizens of Jabesh-gilead, recalling Saul's heroism in saving them from the Ammonites (see page 67), crossed the Jordan at night. They removed the bodies and buried them reverently in Jabesh. Many years later David removed the remains to the sepulchre of Kish at Zelah.

The sad tidings were brought to David at Ziklag by an Amalekite. Trying to please David, he claimed to have dealt the last fatal blow, and produced Saul's crown and armlet. David and his men could not control their grief, and mourned the whole day. Then he sent for the Amalekite and had him put to death for confessing to the murder of God's anointed.

David's famous lament over Saul and Jonathan is one of the earliest and finest of all elegies, and provides a striking example of David's noble character. A less generous heart might have ignored the memory of an unjust master. But David paid tribute to one who had been selected by God to be the first king of Israel. 'Saul and Jonathan, the lovely and the pleasant

78

in their lives, even in their death they were not divided; they were swifter than eagles, they were stronger than lions . . . how are the mighty fallen!'

———————➤•◀———————

Readings from the Bible

I Samuel, chapter 17, verses 32 to 54	David challenges Goliath
I Samuel, chapter 20, verses 18 to 42	Jonathan warns David
I Samuel, chapter 24	David spares Saul's life
I Samuel, chapter 31	Saul's death

Exercises

1. Draw a map and insert the places where David lived as an outlaw.
2. It has been said that Saul was himself largely responsible for the ruin of his career. Comment on this statement, by referring to incidents in Saul's life.
3. Can you think of any reasons why Jonathan realized he would not succeed his father as king?
4. Describe three of David's adventures, during his flight from Saul.

12

REIGN OF DAVID

Part I

David is proclaimed king

SAUL, whose reign lasted for about fifteen years (*c.* 1025 - 1010 B.C.E.), had failed to free his country from the Philistines, who were now in complete control. The Israelites were, however, allowed to conduct their internal affairs as long as they continued to pay tribute to their overlords. The men of Judah turned naturally to David as their new leader. Having received Divine guidance, David left Ziklag for Hebron, where he was proclaimed king of Judah. David was thirty years old at the time and he reigned in Hebron for seven and a half years (*c.* 1010 - 1003 B.C.E.). David's first act after his accession was to convey his thanks to the men of Jabesh-gilead for their pious act in burying the remains of Saul and his sons. The other tribes remained loyal to Ishbosheth, Saul's only surviving son, who had escaped from the battle of Gilboa together with Abner, Saul's cousin and commander-in-chief. Ishbosheth was proclaimed king by Abner at Mahanaim, north of the Jabbok across the Jordan.

Abner kills David's nephew, Asahel

Civil war between the two rival parties was inevitable and the first encounter took place at Gibeon, in Benjamite territory. Ishbosheth's army was led by Abner, and David's by his nephew Joab, the son of his sister Zeruiah, who was accompanied by his brothers Abishai and Asahel. After a fierce engagement, Joab defeated his opponents, who fled from the battlefield, but Abner was closely pursued by Asahel, 'as light of foot as one of the roes that are in the field'. Abner, wishing to avoid a blood-feud, pleaded unsuccessfully with Asahel to turn back, and when he refused, pierced him through with his spear. The pursuit after Abner's routed army continued, and although both sides eventually agreed to a truce, Joab waited for the opportunity to avenge his brother's death.

Abner is murdered by Joab

The civil war continued for some years, with a constantly increasing advantage to the side of David. The climax was reached when Ishbosheth accused Abner, who had married one of Saul's wives, of having designs on the throne. In fierce anger, Abner reproached Ishbosheth, a mere puppet in his hands, for his ingratitude, and swore to transfer the kingdom to David. He immediately made direct overtures to David who agreed to enter into negotiations, provided his former wife, Michal, was restored to him (see page 73). This condition was accepted, and, with the approval of the elders of Israel, Abner went in person to Hebron with a guard of only twenty men. Having been welcomed and feasted, he undertook to win over all Israel to David's side, and departed in peace. At this moment, Joab returned to Hebron from a foray, and on hearing what had happened, was angry with the king and accused Abner of being a spy. Without David's knowledge, he had the unsuspecting Abner brought back to Hebron and stabbed him to death as he entered the gate.

David was enraged at this foul deed, yet he knew he was powerless to punish the assassin on whom he must rely to establish his kingdom — 'These men, the sons of Zeruiah, are too hard for me'. Abner was buried in Hebron, and the king himself followed the bier. Joab, too, was commanded to attend the funeral. Ishbosheth, left helpless by Abner's death, was murdered by two of his captains who carried his head to David at Hebron. They met with the same fate as the Amalekite who brought the news of Saul's death, and were executed.

David becomes king of all Israel

The only remaining claimant to Saul's throne was Mephibosheth, the lame twelve-year-old child of Jonathan, who obviously could command no support. The times required a strong leader who would expel the Philistines, and a deputation of elders from all the tribes offered David the crown. David was now king of all Israel, and the three-day festivities following his coronation were attended by thousands of warriors who had come from all parts of the country.

Jerusalem becomes the capital of Israel

David lost no time in securing the undivided allegiance of all his people. He achieved this by resolving to transfer his capital in Hebron to the Jebusite stronghold of Jerusalem. Its great advantages were obvious. The strongly fortified city lay on the border between Judah and Benjamin, and was centrally situated for governing both the north and the south. It stood on a hill, and was surrounded on three sides by steep ravines. The Jebusites were a warlike race which had occupied Canaan long before Joshua's invasion. They were so convinced their city could never be taken that they boasted it was sufficient to defend it with the blind and lame. David promised high honours to the man who captured the fortress. The courageous Joab, with a few picked men, clambered through a horizontal tunnel which ran from the spring of Gihon, just outside the walls, into the heart of the city, and then climbed the vertical shaft through which the garrison hauled up their water supply. The Jebusites were taken by surprise and surrendered.

(This water tunnel, known as 'Warren's shaft' after its discoverer, was excavated in the year 1867). The hill on which Jerusalem stood was named Mount Zion, and Jerusalem itself became known as 'the city of David'. The king fortified its walls and built a royal palace with the help of Phoenician workmen sent by Hiram, king of Tyre.

When the Philistines heard that David had captured Jerusalem they were determined to prevent him becoming too

David's Tower, Jerusalem

powerful. They immediately invaded Judah, and occupied the valley of Rephaim, south-west of Jerusalem. David took up his position in one of the strongholds, probably in Adullam, and launched a successful counter-offensive. Undeterred, the Philistines made a second attempt, but this time David attacked them from the rear and drove them back, with enormous losses, to Gezer.

The ark is removed to Jerusalem

Jerusalem was firmly established as the capital but David was anxious for it to become the nation's religious centre as well. He therefore made arrangements for the ark to be brought from the house of Abinadab, where it had remained since its restoration by the Philistines (see page 65). The king himself went to Kiryath-jearim, and together with representatives of all the tribes, accompanied the ark with music and singing. The ark was placed on a new cart, driven by Uzzah and Ahio, Abinadab's two sons. As the procession wended its way, the oxen stumbled and Uzzah took hold of the ark to steady it. He was punished for his rashness by instant death, for the ark had to be treated with great reverence as a symbol of God's presence and should have been borne on the Levites' shoulders. In view of this incident, David decided to leave the ark in the house of Obed-edom, the Gittite, a Levite of Gath-rimmon.

After three months, hearing that the ark had proved a source of blessing to Obed-edom's household, David prepared for its final transfer to Jerusalem. On this occasion, David requested Zadok and Abiathar the priests, as well as the chief Levites, to make the necessary preparations. The ark was carried on the Levites' shoulders and brought in triumph to the capital. The king, dancing and singing, headed the procession but Michal, his wife, watching him from the palace window, ridiculed him for his undignified conduct. David replied that no expression of joy to honour God was degrading.

David felt it was unbecoming for the ark to remain in a tent while he himself lived in a palatial dwelling built of cedar. The prophet Nathan, whom he consulted, stated in God's name that David's son, who would succeed him, would build a permanent dwelling-place for the ark, under more peaceful conditions. David had yet to undertake numerous wars which would involve the shedding of blood, but he was assured that he would be victorious and establish a permanent dynasty. The king, in a prayer of thanksgiving, gratefully acknowledged God's goodness towards him.

David's genius in administering his kingdom

David's success in uniting the people and overcoming all enemy opposition was due, in no small measure, to his own brilliant powers of organization. The constitution which he laid down for his kingdom covered every aspect of military, civil and religious administration. We shall deal briefly with each of these.

The armed forces

Joab was the commander-in-chief of all the forces. The standing army consisted of twelve divisions of twenty-four thousand soldiers each, under their own officer. The king's personal bodyguard was recruited from the Cherethites and Pelethites, probably foreign mercenaries, who were commanded by Benaiah the son of Jehoiada. Finally, there was a special unit known as the 'Gibborim', i.e., valiant men, consisting of six hundred selected warriors divided into three groups of two hundred each, under the general command of Abishai, Joab's brother.

The civil heads

The king headed the civil administration assisted by a council of advisers, among whom were Ahitophel and Hushai, of whom we shall hear later, as well as Joab, his commander-in-chief. The court officials included the royal scribe, historian and chief treasurer. A number of judges, mainly Levites, were appointed to administer justice, with the right of appeal to the king himself.

Priests, Levites and Prophets

The principal priests were Zadok and Abiathar, both descendants of Aaron the first High Priest. Zadok ministered in the tabernacle at Gibeon, and Abiathar before the ark at Jerusalem. The Levites, as in the days of Moses, assisted the priests in carrying out their duties, and a Levitical choir was formed to render songs of praise and thanksgiving during divine worship. The three families of Asaph, Heman and Jeduthun were specially chosen for this purpose (the names of these leaders are to be found in the titles of particular psalms). The king, throughout his life, composed numerous hymns to mark

84

particular occasions. Of the one hundred and fifty psalms in the Bible, seventy-three are stated to be written by or for king David. His spiritual advisers were the prophets Gad, who had joined him in exile, and Nathan, who courageously reproved him when the occasion demanded.

David takes steps to protect the country's frontiers

David was determined to destroy the power of surrounding nations in order to protect his country's frontiers against possible invaders. He first launched an attack against the Philistines in the south-west, and captured Gath together with its neighbouring towns. The Amalekites, Edomites, Moabites and Ammonites all fell under his onslaught, as well as the Aramean kingdom of Zobah in the north. Their main cities were garrisoned by David's troops, and enormous quantities of brass, silver and gold were carried off as booty to Jerusalem, later to be used in the construction of the Temple.

Hanun, king of Ammon, insults David

During these campaigns the greatest resistance came from the kingdom of Ammon, towards which David was, at first, well-disposed. He sent ambassadors to Hanun, the new Ammonite king, whose father had died, to offer his condolences. Hanun, influenced by his advisers, treated them as spies and sent them back with half their beards shaved off. When David heard of this outrage he ordered Joab to take vengeance. The Ammonites, although assisted by their Syrian allies, proved no match for the Israelite forces and fled to their capital, Rabbah. The defeated Syrians regrouped their troops but this time David himself crossed the Jordan with his army and put them to flight. The Syrians eventually transferred their allegiance to David.

The prophet Nathan condemns David for his sin

The next year Joab resumed the campaign against the Ammonites and besieged Rabbah, their capital. David, remaining in Jerusalem, committed an indefensible crime which was to have serious consequences. He fell in love with Bathsheba, the wife of Uriah the Hittite, who was away at the battle front. The king recalled Uriah to Jerusalem and sent him back with a sealed letter to Joab, containing the following message, 'Set Uriah in the forefront of the hottest battle, and retire from him, that he may be smitten, and die'. The plot was successful, and after the customary mourning for her husband, Bathsheba became David's wife.

David's shameful conduct was condemned by Nathan the prophet, who made the king realize the enormity of his crime by means of a parable. The prophet told the story of a rich man who entertained a traveller. He owned abundant flocks and herds yet seized the single ewe lamb belonging to his poor neighbour, to provide the meal for the guest. David immediately reacted by declaring that such a man deserved to die. In a few simple but effective words — 'Thou art the man' — Nathan brought the lesson home. He then pronounced the Divine judgment — evil would come to David from the members of his own family. The king frankly admitted his sin against God and, in a psalm which he composed at this time, pleaded for forgiveness. Very soon he suffered the first blow through the death of the baby born to him and Bathsheba. In the course of time a second son was born, whom David called Solomon, 'the peaceful'. Nathan gave the child another name, Jedidiah, 'beloved of God', as a sign of God's favour to both father and child.

In the meantime, Joab was on the point of capturing Rabbah, and invited the king to lead the final assault. David did so and the city was speedily captured. Triumphantly the Israelite army returned to Jerusalem carrying with them much spoil, including the crown of Malcam, the Ammonite god, which was adorned with precious stones.

Readings from the Bible

II Samuel, chapter 5, verses 6 to 10	Capture of Jerusalem
II Samuel, chapter 6, verses 1 to 19	The ark is removed to Jerusalem
II Samuel, chapter 12, verses 1 to 14	Nathan's parable
Psalm 51	David's prayer for forgiveness

Exercises

1. Why was Hebron chosen by David as his first capital?
2. Mention three of the steps taken by David to strengthen his kingdom. Write a short note on each.
3. Give an account of Nathan's parable and explain its application.
4. Write briefly on the following:
   (*a*) Abner; (*b*) Mount Zion; (*c*) Uriah the Hittite.

13

REIGN OF DAVID

Part II

Absalom takes revenge on Amnon

THE second part of David's reign was clouded by a series of crises within his own family circle. David had married several wives, and three of his sons were to cause him much grief. These were his eldest, Amnon; his third, Absalom; and his fourth, Adonijah — all half-brothers. Amnon fell in love with Absalom's sister, Tamar, and behaved in a most offensive manner towards her. David, although angered at Amnon's conduct, took no steps to punish his eldest son, but Absalom waited for an opportunity for revenge. Two years later, he invited all his brothers to a sheep-shearing festival, and, at a pre-arranged signal, his servants killed Amnon while he was the worse for wine. Absalom's brothers fled home in terror and the unhappy father mourned the loss of yet a second son. Absalom took refuge with his grandfather Talmai, the king of Geshur, a small kingdom in the province of Bashan.

Three years later, Joab, noticing how David yearned for his son, took steps to bring about a reconciliation. He employed a 'wise woman' of Tekoa to appear before the king in widow's weeds and present a fictitious petition. One of her two sons, she said, killed the other in a quarrel, and now her family demanded his death, which would leave her childless. David was deeply moved and promised her and her son full protection. The woman then applied the facts of her story to the case of Absalom. Why did not the king, she asked, show a similar compassion for his own son and bring him back from exile? David soon ascertained from the woman that Joab had sent her and gave him permission to bring Absalom back. The king, however, refused to see his son until two years later, when again Joab pleaded for Absalom's restoration to favour.

Before long Absalom showed his true character, for he began craftily to plot against the throne. He had an attractive appearance and impressed the people by riding about in a chariot with fifty men running before him. At the city gate he spoke to people who were coming to plead before the king, and hinted that there would be unnecessary delay in dealing with their cases. Were he to be appointed as judge, he continued, matters would be different — 'so Absalom stole the hearts of the men of Israel'. In this way he gained numerous supporters, especially among those who were discontented with the way David organized things.

As soon as he felt the time was ripe for open revolt, Absalom asked David for permission to go to Hebron in Judah, where he wished to fulfil a vow he had taken and offer a sacrifice. Hebron, it will be recalled, was once David's capital, and the men of Judah still resented the transfer of authority to Jerusalem. Absalom succeeded in gaining many adherents who joined in the plot to overthrow David. Within a short time, he sent messengers throughout the land to inform his supporters that at a given signal they were to acclaim him as their king. Ahitophel, Bathsheba's grandfather, and one of David's most able counsellors, turned out to be a traitor. At Absalom's invitation, he joined him at Hebron. The revolt began and news of the conspiracy reached the capital. David realized that he was powerless against any sudden attack, and fled from Jerusalem. He was accompanied by many loyal subjects, including his personal bodyguard and six hundred Gittite warriors who had enlisted in his army. Zadok and Abiathar, as well as the Levites carrying the ark, accompanied David part of the way, but then returned at his request. The priests could be of greater service to David in the city by advising him of Absalom's plans.

On the summit of the Mount of Olives, which David ascended on his route towards the Jordan valley, he was met by Hushai, his good friend and adviser. David told him also to return and offer his services to Absalom. In this way he could defeat any advice Ahitophel might give to Absalom, and pass on any information to Zadok and Abiathar.

In the meantime, Absalom had entered Jerusalem and called on his counsellors for their advice. Ahitophel proposed that Absalom provide him with an army of twelve thousand men — he would then fall upon David that very night while the king was weak and dispirited. This advice was generally approved but Hushai, called upon for his view, thought such an attempt would be rash, as the enemy was so strong. Absalom should rather wait and summon all Israel to his aid and then attack David with an overwhelming force. Absalom accepted Hushai's plan and the humiliated Ahitophel went home and hanged himself. Hushai immediately informed Zadok and Abiathar of Absalom's decision and they sent their sons to warn David, who was now waiting in the Jordan valley. The king and his forces crossed the river Jordan and David took up his residence at Mahanaim, the former capital of Ishbosheth. Absalom appointed Amasa as commander of his main forces and then he, too, crossed the Jordan.

David prepared for battle with his usual skill and divided his army into three divisions under Joab, Abishai and Ittai the Gittite, who was one of his most devoted followers. The king remained in the city, but as his three captains left for the battlefield he issued the command, 'deal gently for my sake with the young man, even with Absalom'. The battle took place in the dense forest, and Absalom's army was defeated with a loss of twenty thousand men. Absalom, mounted on a mule, endeavoured to escape but his long and flowing hair became entangled in the lower branches of an oak, and left him suspended in the air. Informed of this, Joab hastened to the spot and pierced Absalom's heart with his darts. The final death blow was delivered by ten of Joab's soldiers. Absalom's body was thrown into a pit and covered with a heap of stones.

The old king waited impatiently at Mahanaim for news. When he heard that his son was dead, he broke down completely and returned to his house weeping, 'O my son Absalom, my son, my son Absalom! Would I had died for thee, O Absalom, my son, my son!' The king's grief turned the victory into mourning and the soldiers stole away to their quarters as if vanquished. Only Joab dared speak boldly and rebuked David for discouraging his friends, who would desert him if he did not change his attitude. This aroused David from his despondency and, in spite of his distress, he appeared at the city gate to receive the people.

David returns to
Jerusalem

The revolt was over, and the Israelites wished their king to return to his capital. The men of Judah, who had supported Absalom, were naturally worried as to how the king would react towards them. David again displayed his political genius by sending his two faithful priests, Zadok and Abiathar, to the elders of Judah, urging them not to be the last to recall him. David promised to appoint Amasa, who had commanded Absalom's forces, as captain in the place of the headstrong Joab. The men of Judah were won over and invited the king to cross the Jordan. They met him at the ancient camp at Gilgal, and escorted him to Jerusalem.

Sheba, the
Benjamite, rebels

The prominence given to the men of Judah excited the jealousy of the other tribes, and Sheba, a Benjamite, rallied them round his standard and revolted. The king ordered his new captain, Amasa, to muster the forces of Judah within three days and crush the rebellion. Amasa failed to do so in the allotted time so Abishai was ordered to take over and Joab accompanied him. When the army reached Gibeon, Joab found that Amasa had already arrived there. Pretending to embrace him, Joab dealt him a fatal blow with his sword. Sheba fled northwards and took refuge in the town of Abel, where he was besieged by Joab's followers. The inhabitants, to avoid being attacked, took the advice of a 'wise woman' and put Sheba to death. So the war ended and Joab returned to Jerusalem.

David is punished
for numbering the
people

In order to find out the strength of his army, David ordered a census of all the tribes. The reason for his doing so is not clear, but David seems to have been prompted by a desire to boast about his great military strength. This was a grave error on his part, for the real strength of Israel lay in God's protection. Even Joab warned him against such a move, but the king persisted, and Joab and his officers carried out his commission. They completed their task almost ten months later and returned to Jerusalem with the report that Israel had 800,000 men fit for military service and Judah, 500,000.

As soon as the final census had been taken, David realized he had sinned, and prayed for forgiveness. The prophet Gad, in God's name, announced a punishment of either seven years' famine or three months' flight before his enemies or an outbreak of a plague lasting three days. The king chose the latter and a pestilence broke out killing seventy thousand people throughout the land from Dan to Beersheba. Whilst the plague was raging in Jerusalem, David had a vision of an angel stretching out a drawn sword towards the city. David prayed that Jerusalem be spared any punishment and was told by the prophet Gad to build an altar on the spot where the angel had been seen. This was occupied by the threshing floor of Araunah, one of the old Jebusites of the city. David purchased the threshing floor where he built an altar and offered sacrifices — the plague then ceased. This altar marked the sacred spot where the Temple was later built.

Solomon is named as David's heir

David was growing old and felt his end was near. He designated Solomon, his youngest son, as his successor, and told him that it would be his privilege to build God's house. David began to make preparations by amassing treasures and materials to be used eventually for building the Temple.

Adonijah claims the throne

The announcement of Solomon as David's successor put an end to the hopes of Adonijah, who had designs on the throne. Taking advantage of his father's advanced age, Adonijah resolved to make himself king. Like Absalom, he rode about in a chariot with fifty men running before him. Moreover he won over Joab and Abiathar to his side. Zadok, the priest, Benaiah, the captain of David's bodyguard, and the prophet Nathan remained faithful to the king. Whilst Adonijah was entertaining members of the royal family and chief nobles at a banquet, the prophet Nathan informed Bathsheba of what had occurred and she immediately passed the news on to the king. At his command, Zadok, Nathan and Benaiah led the young prince, on the king's mule, to the brook of Gihon where Zadok formally anointed Solomon king. The people acclaimed

Solomon as their new monarch and the sound of rejoicing reached the banqueting table of Adonijah. When the guests heard the news of the royal decree, they quickly dispersed, leaving Adonijah entirely deserted. Adonijah fled to the sanctuary and seized the horns of the altar for protection. On Solomon's assurance that his life would be spared if he proved worthy, Adonijah returned to his own house unharmed.

David's last act was to send for Solomon and call on him to keep God's statutes, as written in the law of Moses. David warned his son to be wary of his former enemies, but, on the other hand, to show kindness to his friends. Soon afterwards the king died at the age of seventy, having reigned just over forty years (c. 1010 - 970 B.C.E.), seven and a half years in Hebron and thirty-three in Jerusalem. David was laid to rest in his own beloved capital — the city of Jerusalem.

———————————⟶•⟵———————————

Readings from the Bible

II Samuel, chapter 15, verses 1 to 12 — Absalom's plot
II Samuel, chapter 18, verses 9 to 18 — Absalom's death
I Kings, chapter 1, verses 5 to 31 — Adonijah claims the throne
I Kings, chapter 2, verses 1 to 12 — David's final message to Solomon

Exercises

1. David has been described as 'shepherd, soldier, poet, man of faith, patriot, friend, and devoted father'. Mention an incident in his life which illustrates each of these qualities.
2. Can you suggest why David preferred Solomon as his successor rather than his older brothers?
3. Write briefly on the following:
   (a) The wise woman of Tekoa; (b) Hushai; (c) Adonijah.

92

14

REIGN OF SOLOMON

Solomon takes steps to secure his throne

SOLOMON was a young man when he became king, probably no more than eighteen years of age, and he reigned for forty years (*c.* 970 - 930 B.C.E.). He was immediately faced with yet another attempt by Adonijah to assert his claim to the throne. According to ancient custom, the wives of a deceased king passed with his property to his successor. Adonijah had the audacity to ask for permission to marry Abishag, the Shunammite, his father's latest wife. Solomon was convinced that his elder brother, supported by Joab and Abiathar, still considered himself to be the rightful heir. At the king's command, Adonijah was executed by Benaiah, formerly one of David's captains (see page 84). But Abiathar, in consideration of his sacred office and former loyalty to David when he fled from Saul, was deposed from the priesthood and banished to his home at Anathoth. Joab fled to the Tabernacle and caught hold of the horns of the altar for protection but this did not save him. Solomon, recalling how Joab had murdered Abner and Amasa (see pages 81 and 90), ordered Benaiah to put him to death. Benaiah was appointed commander-in-chief of the army in Joab's place and Zadok assumed the office of High Priest. Solomon was now free from trouble within his kingdom and could devote himself almost entirely to affairs of state.

The young king prays for wisdom

Solomon took an early opportunity of worshipping in the Tabernacle at Gibeon, where he offered numerous sacrifices. During the night he had a remarkable dream, for he heard

God's voice saying 'Ask what I shall give thee'. The young king prayed simply for an understanding heart to enable him to distinguish between right and wrong, and so fit him for the responsible task of judging his people. Because he had not selfishly asked for riches or victory over his enemies, these were granted to him in addition. When Solomon returned to Jerusalem he expressed his gratitude to God by offering sacrifices before the ark and invited his courtiers to a celebration.

An occasion soon presented itself to test his wisdom. Two women appeared before him, each of whom had recently given birth to a child. One of the babies had died and its mother now claimed the living child as her own. Calling for a sword, the king told one of his guards to divide the living child in two, and give half to one woman and half to the other. The true mother immediately pleaded that the child's life be spared and that it be given to the other, whilst the false mother agreed to the king's proposal. Solomon had no difficulty in deciding the dispute. News of his judgment spread through all Israel and the people paid homage to their gifted king.

Solomon became famous for his wisdom and, during his lifetime, composed three thousand proverbs and one thousand and five songs. In them he spoke 'of trees . . . of beasts, and of fowl, and of creeping things, and of fishes'. Many of his sayings are probably preserved in the three books of the Bible ascribed to him: The Book of Proverbs; The Song of Songs; and Ecclesiastes.

Solomon maintains a luxurious court

Solomon organized his military, civil and religious administration on the same lines as his father before him (see page 84), but on a scale of much greater splendour. He was particularly lavish in the maintenance of his court. The daily provision of food alone amounted to thirty measures of fine flour, sixty measures of meal, thirty oxen, and one hundred sheep, besides venison and fowl. In his military establishment, he possessed forty thousand stalls of horses for his one thousand four hundred chariots, all purchased from Egypt. The country was divided into twelve districts each administered by an officer who collected the required provisions and funds for one month in the year. These contributions were increased by the tribute of all the subject kingdoms between the Euphrates, the eastern

94

border of Solomon's dominions, to the Egyptian frontier. Judah and Israel were indeed prosperous and 'every man dwelt safely under his vine and under his fig-tree, from Dan even to Beersheba, all the days of Solomon'.

The building of the Temple

Solomon's greatest achievement was the building of the Temple. As we have seen, its site had been determined by David, who made some preliminary preparations (see page 91). Hiram, king of Tyre, sent delegates to Solomon to congratulate him on his accession, and readily agreed to assist in providing workmen and materials for the construction of God's house. A treaty was entered into whereby Hiram provided cedar and fir trees from Lebanon to be floated to the port of Jaffa by Phoenician sailors. He also supplied skilled craftsmen, led by an outstanding expert, also named Hiram, to design and fashion the necessary brass work. In exchange, Solomon sent the Phoenicians, each year, large quantities of wheat, barley, wine and oil. Solomon called up thirty thousand Israelites for compulsory service, and sent them to cut trees in Lebanon in relays of ten thousand, each relay serving for one month, and returning home for two. Besides these, seventy thousand foreign subjects were ordered to work as porters, eighty thousand as hewers of stones in the quarries, and three thousand six hundred as overseers. Every stone was shaped before it was brought to the sacred site, so avoiding the use of hammer or axe, or any iron tool, as the structure rose.

The foundation stone was laid in the fourth year of Solomon's reign (*c.* 967 B.C.E.) in the month of Ziv (Iyyar) and the actual construction took seven and a half years. The Temple was a permanent structure made of stone. The roof was covered with planks of cedar, and the whole house was overlaid with gold. Three storeys of small rooms, where the sacred vessels were kept, were built around its sides.

The courtyard

As in the Sanctuary, the Temple consisted of three parts: The courtyard; the Holy Place; and the Holy of Holies (see page 30). In the courtyard, which surrounded the Temple, stood the altar of burnt-offering and the brass 'sea', a masterpiece of Hiram's skill, where the priests washed before they performed their duties. It was so called because of its great size, being

95

seven and a half feet high and fifteen feet in diameter. It rested on the backs of twelve brass oxen, arranged in sets of three, each set facing one of the points of the compass. In addition there were ten smaller lavers used for cleansing purposes.

The Holy Place

Leading into the Holy Place was a Porch, or entrance hall, facing eastward. It measured thirty feet by fifteen feet and was one hundred and eighty feet high so that it towered above the rest of the building. The Porch was adorned by two ornamental brass pillars, also cast by Hiram. These pillars were called Jachin ('He will establish') and Boaz ('In Him lies strength'). The Holy Place, reserved for the priests, was sixty feet long, thirty feet wide and forty-five feet high. In it stood the golden altar of incense, the table of showbread, and ten golden candlesticks. This room had several windows inserted in the walls just below the ceiling.

The Holy of Holies

The Holy of Holies formed a perfect cube, being thirty feet in length, width and height. It contained the Ark and two huge cherubim, fifteen feet high, carved out of olive-wood overlaid with gold; their outstretched wings spanned the entire room.

The Temple is dedicated

The dedication of the Temple took place on the eighth day of the seventh month (Tishri), a week before the commencement of the Feast of Tabernacles, about the year 960 B.C.E. The king and the people waited in the outer court, whilst the priests brought the ark in joyous procession to its permanent resting-place in the Holy of Holies. On the priests' return to the court, the Levites, accompanied by their musical instruments, chanted the psalm, 'For He is good, for His mercy endureth for ever'. At that moment the Temple was filled with a cloud, a visible sign of God's presence. Turning towards the people, Solomon blessed the God of Israel who had fulfilled His promise to David that his son would build the Temple. Then, stretching his hands towards heaven, he entreated that God would answer His people's prayers directed towards the Temple and forgive their sins. Solomon's prayer was followed by yet another sign of God's presence, for fire came down from heaven and consumed the sacrifices. The occasion was celebrated by a seven-days' feast, followed by the seven-days' festival of Tabernacles. On the twenty-third day of the seventh month, the people returned to their homes, 'joyful and glad of heart for the goodness that the Lord had shown unto David, and to Solomon, and to Israel His people'.

During his reign, Solomon had amassed considerable wealth, partly from the tribute nations, partly through his commercial enterprises, but mainly through heavy taxation imposed on his own people. He spent vast sums on constructing his own magnificent palace which took thirteen years to complete and comprised a number of luxurious buildings. These included:

(i) 'the House of the Forest of Lebanon', which measured one hundred and fifty feet by seventy-five feet, and was so called because it was supported by rows of cedar pillars. Among the expensive ornaments adorning this royal residence were two hundred shields overlaid with gold;

(ii) the 'Porch of Pillars', measuring seventy-five feet by forty-five feet, possibly the royal reception room;

(iii) the Throne-room which also served as the Hall of Justice;

(iv) the palace of Pharaoh's daughter, whom he had married to strengthen his ties with Egypt.

Solomon's throne

Solomon spared no expense in furnishing his palace, and all his drinking vessels were made of pure gold. His throne, made of ivory and overlaid with the finest gold, was elevated on six steps, each flanked by a pair of lions made of gold.

With the completion of the Temple and palace, Solomon and Hiram exchanged gifts. The services of the king of Tyre were acknowledged by the gift of twenty cities in Galilee. Hiram was not too pleased, but sent Solomon one hundred and twenty talents of gold.

The king develops trade with other countries

Solomon now turned his attention to fortifying strategic points throughout the country, for example: the walls of Jerusalem; Hazor, in the north; Megiddo, in the valley of Esdraelon; and Gezer, in the south, as well as the cities where he kept his stores and chariots. The importance of establishing trade relations with other countries was not lost on so wise a king. He constructed a fleet of ships, stationed at the port of Ezion-geber, near Elath. Navigated by Hiram's skilled sailors, they sailed to distant countries carrying merchandise and returned with gold, silver, ivory, apes and peacocks. Each voyage took three years to accomplish. Solomon also imported horses and chariots from Egypt for sale to other countries.

Excavations at Ezion-geber have revealed the remains of a copper refinery built about the tenth century B.C.E. There is no reason to doubt that the mining industry flourished in Solomon's days, and provided him with a considerable income.

The Queen of Sheba pays a state visit

Solomon's wisdom and supremacy were universally acknowledged and he was paid a state visit by the Queen of Sheba, a kingdom in the south-west of Arabia. With a large caravan of camels, bearing gold and precious stones and spices, she came to Jerusalem to test the king's skill through difficult questions. The perfect wisdom of the king's replies, the magnificence of his buildings, the splendour of his royal state, all completely overwhelmed the queen. She admitted that she had not believed the reports of his wisdom but now she was fully convinced. Having given and received magnificent presents, she returned to her own country.

Solomon's decline and death

As Solomon grew older, he was influenced more and more by his heathen wives. In addition to Pharaoh's daughter, he married Moabite, Ammonite, Edomite, Phoenician and Hittite women. His wives induced him to provide shrines for their idols, and he no longer worshipped God with a perfect heart. The king received a Divine communication condemning him

98

for his infidelity, the punishment for which would be the partition of the kingdom after his death.

Solomon's last years were troubled by outbreaks of war and revolution. Hadad, an Edomite prince, who had fled to Egypt during David's reign, returned to his own country and began to harass Solomon. A more formidable adversary was Rezon, the Syrian, who seized Damascus in the north. The greatest danger, however, arose from one of his own people, Jeroboam, the son of Nebat, an Ephraimite, who had been employed in strengthening the fortifications of Jerusalem. His ability attracted Solomon's notice and he appointed him as overseer of the labour forces conscripted from the tribe of Ephraim. Soon afterwards, Jeroboam was met by the prophet Ahijah, who tore the new garment he was wearing into twelve pieces, and gave ten of them to Jeroboam. The prophet announced that God would tear the kingdom out of the hand of Solomon, and give ten of the tribes to Jeroboam. The others would be retained by Solomon's heir, for David's sake. The incident was reported to Solomon, who wanted to kill Jeroboam, but the latter fled to Egypt, and remained under the protection of Shishak, king of Egypt, until Solomon's death.

It was indeed a tragedy that a king who had showed such promise should end his years an unhappy and disappointed man. Solomon died at Jerusalem in the fortieth year of his reign, and was buried in the royal sepulchre in the City of David.

———————>•<———————

Readings from the Bible		
	I Kings, chapter 3, verses 4 to 15	Solomon asks for wisdom
	I Kings, chapter 8, verses 22 to 53	Solomon's prayer
	I Kings, chapter 10, verses 1 to 13	The queen of Sheba
	I Kings, chapter 11, verses 26 to 40	Rise of Jeroboam

Exercises

1. Enumerate the main events during Solomon's reign. How did it differ from King David's reign?
2. Give a general description of the Temple. Mention three ways in which it differed from the Tabernacle.
3. When are the 'Song of Songs' and 'the book of Ecclesiastes' read in the Synagogue? Give the reasons.
4. Write briefly on the following:
   (*a*) Hiram, king of Tyre; (*b*) Elath; (*c*) Queen of Sheba.

15

THE COUNTRY IS DIVIDED

A general survey

SHORTLY after Solomon's death, Ahijah's prophecy was fulfilled and the country was divided into two parts forming the separate kingdoms of Judah and Israel. As we shall see, the kingdom of Israel existed for nearly 210 years (c. 930 - 722 B.C.E), whereas that of Judah lasted much longer, for just over 340 years (c. 930 - 586 B.C.E). At first sight this may seem surprising, for the northern kingdom, which included the region east of the Jordan, was almost three times the size of the southern kingdom and could muster a greater army against enemy attack. But from a religious point of view, the kingdom of Judah was by far the stronger, for it retained Jerusalem as its capital, with the Temple as the centre of worship. God's promise to David of a permanent dynasty (see page 83) was fulfilled to the very end, and, from Rehoboam onwards, the crown was handed down, generally from father to son. Although many of Judah's rulers were guilty of idol-worship, a number were outstanding for their piety, such as Asa, Jehoshaphat, Hezekiah and Josiah.

On the other hand, the kings of Israel, with scarcely an exception, 'did that which was evil in the sight of the Lord, and departed not from the sins of Jeroboam, the son of Nebat, wherewith he made Israel to sin'. In fact, Jeroboam's dynasty ended with his son, and future successions were constantly broken by murders and revolutions, so that in all there were five main dynasties. We shall be highlighting the activities of the more prominent kings of Judah and Israel, beginning with the reigns of Rehoboam and Jeroboam.

100

This chapter deals with the first three rulers in both kingdoms as shown in the following chart:

Kings of Judah	Approximate dates of accession, B.C.E.	Kings of Israel	Approximate dates of accession, B.C.E.
Rehoboam	930	Jeroboam I	930
Abijam	913	Nadab	910
Asa	910	Baasa	909

The ten tribes rebel against Rehoboam

Solomon's son Rehoboam succeeded to the throne at the age of forty-one, and selected Shechem, in the territory of Ephraim, as the place for his coronation. This was a shrewd move on his part. The rivalry between the tribe of Judah and the northern tribes in David's reign has already been mentioned (see page 90). By selecting Shechem rather than Jerusalem, Rehoboam hoped to gain the loyalty of all his subjects. Furthermore, the new king must have known of the prophet Ahijah's meeting with Jeroboam, who was an Ephramite (see page 99). He failed to reckon, however, with the growing discontent at the heavy burden of taxation and forced labour imposed by his father. Jeroboam was recalled from Egypt by the leaders of the northern tribes, and led a delegation to demand some relief in return for the people's allegiance. Rehoboam took three days to think the matter over. His late father's experienced counsellors advised a friendly reply but Rehoboam preferred the opinion of the young men who had grown up with him at the court. Urged on by them, he refused the petition by replying, with reckless insolence, 'My father made your yoke heavy, but I will add to your yoke; my father chastised you with whips, but I will chastise you with scorpions'. The reaction was immediate. The leaders of the ten tribes called on their people to rebel and sever all connections with Rehoboam. Adoram, the chief collector of taxes, was sent to restore order but was stoned to death, and Rehoboam escaped only by fleeing in his chariot to Jerusalem.

The rebellion was successful, and Jeroboam was proclaimed king over all Israel at Shechem. The tribes of Judah and Benjamin, however, remained loyal to the house of David and answered Rehoboam's summons to fight the rebels. But the enterprise was forbidden by the prophet Shemaiah, who declared that the separation of the kingdoms was in accordance with God's will. Nevertheless, hostility between the kingdoms of Judah and Israel, as they were now called, continued under Rehoboam and his two successors, until the reign of Ahab.

The Reign of Rehoboam

Rehoboam fortifies his kingdom

The first three years of Rehoboam's reign were peaceful. He made every effort to strengthen his diminished kingdom by fortifying several cities in Judah and Benjamin, and equipped them with arms and stores of food. The king served God faithfully, and large numbers of priests and Levites, whom Jeroboam had removed from office (see page 103), flocked to Jerusalem and resumed their sacred duties in the Temple.

Shishak of Egypt invades Judah

Before long, Rehoboam, probably influenced by his foreign wives, erected pagan shrines throughout his dominion, and both king and people practised the most degrading forms of idolatry. The Divine punishment for this sin came in the form of an attack by Shishak, king of Egypt, the former protector of Jeroboam (see page 99), who led his army against Jerusalem in the fifth year of Rehoboam's reign. Shishak captured the strong cities of Judah, and had reached Jerusalem, when the king and princes, reproved by the prophet Shemaiah, admitted their guilt and repented. Shishak withdrew his forces but took away with him the treasures of the Temple and the royal palace. He also carried off the celebrated golden shields of Solomon (see page 97), which Rehoboam replaced by shields of brass.

An account of Shishak's campaign is recorded on the walls of the great temple at Karnak in upper Egypt. A series of carvings show the king being presented with captives by the god Amon and his goddess. From the names of the captured towns listed on the inscription, it would appear that Shishak invaded Israel as well as Judah.

After ruling for seventeen years, Rehoboam died and was buried in the city of David. He was succeeded by his son Abijam, whose brief reign of three years seems to have been spent in waging war against Jeroboam.

*Jeroboam sets up
pagan shrines in
Dan and Bethel*

Jeroboam, the first king of Israel, began his reign by fortifying Shechem and making it his capital. He later transferred his seat of government to Penuel in Transjordan, and finally to the town of Tirzah. But Jeroboam could not feel secure as long as his subjects continued to flock to Jerusalem on the pilgrim festivals. After some thought, he set up two golden calves, one in Dan and one in Bethel, the extreme north and south of his kingdom, and called on his people to visit these shrines rather than make the long journey to Jerusalem. He appointed priests from the masses, in place of the Levites, who consequently went to Jerusalem (see page 102). Bethel became the chief centre, and the king proclaimed a feast of dedication on the fifteenth day of the eighth month, in imitation of the dedication of the Temple at the feast of tabernacles (see page 96), but a month later, 'in the month which he had devised of his own heart'.

As Jeroboam was about to offer incense, he was confronted by a man of God who prophesied that Josiah, a descendant of David, would one day burn the bones of the idolatrous priests on the altar. The enraged king called on his guards to seize the prophet, and put out his own hand to lay hold of him, but the hand became paralysed and fell helpless at his side. In response to Jeroboam's earnest plea, the prophet prayed for the king's hand to be restored, but refused to accept any reward, and departed. The warning had no permanent effect on Jeroboam, who persisted in his idolatrous worship, and consecrated any one as a priest who could afford to bring an offering of a young bullock and seven rams.

*Jeroboam is punished
by the death of
his son*

The Divine punishment was severe. His son Abijah, the only one of his house 'in whom there was found some good thing toward the Lord, the God of Israel', fell ill and Jeroboam sent his wife to consult the aged prophet Ahijah, who was almost blind. Though the queen disguised herself by wearing ordinary clothes, Ahijah knew immediately who she was. He recalled all Jeroboam's sins and foretold the speedy end of his dynasty. The child was to die, but, as a reward for his piety, he alone of all his house would be buried in peace. The queen returned to Tirzah, and the child died as she crossed the threshold. He was buried and lamented by all Israel. Jeroboam died after a reign of twenty-two years and was buried in the sepulchre of his fathers. He was succeeded by his son Nadab.

Nadab had been on the throne for only two years when he became the victim of a military conspiracy. Baasa, probably one of his captains, killed the king and massacred all the house of Jeroboam, so fulfilling the prophecy of Ahijah.

The Reigns of Asa and Baasa

Asa of Judah and Baasa of Israel were contemporaries. Asa, the third king of Judah, succeeded his father Abijam and reigned for forty-one years, Baas, the third king of Israel, reigned at Tirzah for twenty-four years.

The pious Asa and his religious reforms

Asa, a man of great piety, lost no time in destroying every trace of idolatry. He even deposed his mother Maachah from the rank of queen-mother for making an image. During the earlier part of his reign, Asa fortified his frontier towns and raised an army of 580,000 men, of whom 300,000 were men of Judah, armed with spears and shields, and 280,000 Benjamite archers. This military preparation may have been connected with an attempt to throw off the tributary yoke which Shishak had imposed upon Rehoboam (see page 102), and it brought upon Asa the whole force of the Egyptian army. Zerah, the Ethiopian, probably one of Shishak's captains, invaded Judah, but Asa confronted him at Mareshah in the south-west of Judah and, after a fervent prayer to God, routed the enemy forces and pursued them to Gerar. He returned to Jerusalem with abundant spoil and innumerable sheep and cattle.

The prophet Azariah met Asa on his return, and urged him and his subjects to be firm in their loyalty to God. His words resulted in a new and more thorough reformation. The idols were removed from all the cities of Judah and Benjamin, and Asa called a great assembly at Jerusalem, in the third month of the fifteenth year of his reign. It was attended not only by the people of Judah and Benjamin, but by members of Ephraim, Manasseh, and other tribes who, dissatisfied with Baasa, had come to live in Judah. The large assembly took an oath to

104

serve God with all their hearts, and to punish any idolater with death.

Asa, with Syrian aid, compels Baasa to lift his blockade

Baasa was alarmed at the number of his own people who crossed the border. He therefore attempted to blockade the frontier by fortifying the town of Ramah, a few miles north of Jerusalem, to prevent his subjects deserting to Asa. It was then that the good king of Judah committed the one great error of his life. He called for the help of Benhadad I, the Syrian king of Damascus, to invade the northern territory of Israel, and purchased his alliance by giving him all the silver and gold left in the royal palace. Benhadad's invasion had the desired effect. Baasa withdrew his forces from the city of Ramah, and he does not appear to have renewed the attack. When Baasa died, he was buried in Tirzah, leaving the kingdom to his son Elah.

Asa's lack of faith in relying on Syria rather than on God was reproved by the seer Hanani, who foretold that he would be troubled by constant war for the rest of his days. The enraged king ordered the seer to be imprisoned. Towards the end of his life, Asa suffered from a serious foot disease which seems to have caused his death. His son Jehoshaphat, who probably acted as regent for a time, succeeded him.

Readings from the Bible

I Kings, chapter 12, verses 1 to 20   Revolt of the ten tribes
I Kings, chapter 12, verses 25 to 33   Jeroboam sets up two golden calves
II Chronicles, chapter 16   Asa's war with Baasa

Exercises

1. Trace the events which led to the division of the Kingdom. What were the results?
2. Why was there such enmity between the tribes of Judah and Israel?
3. Give an account of Jeroboam's reign.
4. Mention two important events in Asa's reign. Write briefly on each of them.

16

THE HOUSE OF OMRI

Part I

Kings of Judah	Approximate dates of accession, B.C.E.	Kings of Israel	Approximate dates of accession, B.C.E.
		Elah	886
		Zimri	885
Jehoshaphat	873	Omri	885
		Ahab	874
Jehoram	849	Ahaziah	853
Ahaziah	842	Jehoram	852

A brief glance at the reigns of Elah and Zimri

IN this chapter we shall be dealing mainly with the contrasting personalities of the courageous prophet Elijah and the weak-kneed Ahab, king of Israel. We shall also refer to Ahab's contemporary, king Jehoshaphat of Judah. But let us first sketch the developments following Baasa's death, recorded in the last chapter. His son Elah, the fourth king of Israel, seems to have been an incompetent ruler. While his troops were waging war against the Philistines, he remained in his palace at Tirzah enjoying a life of ease and luxury. In the second year of his reign he and all the members of his household were assassinated by Zimri, one of his captains, who occupied the throne for only seven days. The army, refusing to recognize Zimri, elected their general, Omri, as king, and immediately marched against Tirzah. Zimri, seeing that he was about to be captured, set fire to the palace and perished in the flames. The claim of Omri to the throne was disputed by another competitor named Tibni, who received substantial support, but he died after a civil war lasting five years.

The Reign of Omri

Omri chooses Samaria as his capital

Omri, the sixth king of Israel, reigned for twelve years. The Bible tells us only that he was as sinful as his predecessors and that he transferred his capital from Tirzah to Samaria. Samaria, so called after a man named Shemer from whom Omri bought the site for two talents of silver, stood on the crest of a conical hill, three hundred feet above the level of the surrounding valley. We know, however, from other records that Omri's life was far more eventful. He conquered the country of Moab, which became tributary to Israel for many years (see page 119) and is the first Hebrew king to be mentioned in Assyrian inscriptions where Israel is described as 'the land of the house of Omri'. He was less successful in his wars with Syria, for a number of towns belonging to the northern kingdom seem to have been seized by the enemy (see page 112). On his death, he was succeeded by his son Ahab.

The Reigns of Ahab and Jehoshaphat

Ahab, under Jezebel's influence, introduces Baal worship

Ahab, the seventh king of Israel, reigned for twenty-two years. Politically he was most astute. Realizing that the Syrians in the north were the main danger to his country, Ahab concluded a peace treaty with his contemporary, Jehoshaphat of Judah, in case his help would be needed. Furthermore, like Solomon before him, he saw the advantage of an alliance with the Phoenicians, and married Jezebel, the daughter of Ethbaal, king of the Zidonians. This marriage was to prove disastrous, for as a result of the queen's evil influence, Baal-worship was established throughout Israel. Ahab built a temple in Samaria in honour of the idol and erected a grove for the impure orgies of the goddess Astarte. The four hundred and fifty prophets of Baal and the four hundred of Astarte were maintained at Jezebel's table. By her orders, the true prophets of God were put to death; only a hundred managed to escape her wrath, through the intervention of the God-fearing Obadiah, the royal overseer, who hid and fed them in a cave.

Jehoshaphat, the fourth king of Judah, in complete contrast to Ahab, loathed any form of idol-worship. He was as pious as his father, Asa, and banned the erection of heathen shrines. In the third year of his reign he appointed a royal commission, consisting of his chief princes and selected Levites and priests, to visit his cities and spread the knowledge of God's law among his people. His piety was rewarded with prosperity and he maintained peaceful relations with his neighbours. Even the Philistines paid him tribute in the form of gifts of silver, and the Arabians brought him large numbers of rams and goats. He utilized his wealth to fortify his important cities, and maintained a large standing army. We have already mentioned his alliance with the kingdom of Israel, which was eventually strengthened by the marriage of his son, Jehoram, to Athaliah, the daughter of Ahab and Jezebel. Before describing Jehoshaphat's and Ahab's joint attack against Benhadad of Syria, which took place towards the end of Ahab's reign (see page 113), we shall turn our attention to one of the most striking and challenging figures in Jewish history — Elijah, the Tishbite.

The spiritual decline of the entire nation of Israel was dramatically arrested by the sudden appearance of the prophet Elijah, who had left his native town of Tishbe, in Gilead, to confront the king. In God's name, Elijah announced that Ahab's sinful conduct would be punished by a severe drought, to last several years. Having delivered his message, Elijah fled from the king's presence and hid himself near the brook Cherith. There he was fed with bread and meat brought to him by ravens, and there he remained until the brook dried up.

Forced to find another hiding place, he was divinely directed to go to Zarephath, a Phoenician city. At the city gate, he found a poor widow gathering sticks — a victim of the famine caused by the lack of rain. She was about to prepare a meal for herself and her son from her last handful of meal and drop of oil. The prophet told her not to fear, but to bake a small cake for himself first, and assured her that the meal and oil would not fail as long as the famine lasted. The widow carried out the prophet's request and miraculously they all managed to sustain themselves with food, throughout the drought.

After some time the widow's son became seriously ill and was at death's door. In her grief, she attributed the tragedy to Elijah, as though his presence had caused her to be punished for some past sin. The prophet carried the boy up to his room, and prayed to God that his life be spared. The lad revived, and the grateful mother acknowledged Elijah as a true son of God.

Elijah challenges the Baal prophets on Mount Carmel

After three years had elapsed, Elijah was told by God to leave his hiding place and announce to Ahab the end of the drought. The drought had proved so disastrous that it was impossible to find enough grass to save the lives of the king's horses and cattle. Ahab left his royal palace in Samaria and undertook the search for fodder in person, going in one direction while Obadiah, the royal overseer, went in another. Obadiah was met by Elijah, and after being assured that the prophet would not suddenly vanish, took the risk of announcing his reappearance to Ahab. The king met Elijah with the threatening question, 'Art thou he that troubleth Israel?' — but the prophet blamed the cause of the famine on the king's idolatry. He then challenged Ahab to arrange a decisive trial between God and Baal, on the heights of Mount Carmel.

On the one side were Baal's prophets, supported by the court and followed by the people. On the other, Elijah stood alone, and proposed a test of the simplest kind; that each party should prepare a bullock and lay it on wood, and pray to their respective gods to send down fire upon the sacrifice — 'The god that answereth by fire, let him be God'. All the people assented to so fair a trial. Elijah gave Baal's prophets the first choice. At early morn they prepared the sacrifice, and the air resounded till high noon with their wild cries of 'O Baal, hear us!' But there was no response and they leaped about their altar. As evening approached, Elijah taunted them with the words, 'Cry aloud! For he is a god! either he is musing, or he has gone aside, or he is on a journey, or peradventure he sleepeth and must be awaked'. The priests renewed their cries, and cut their flesh with knives according to their custom, till their blood streamed down. But there was not a sign that their god so much as noticed them.

As the hour of the evening sacrifice drew near, Elijah built an altar of twelve stones, corresponding to the twelve tribes.

Having made a trench round the altar, he laid the bullock on the wood and told the bystanders to pour water over the animal and wood until they were thoroughly drenched. Elijah prayed to God to show His might and fire came down from heaven in sight of all the people, consuming not only the sacrifice and the wood, but the very stones and dust of the altar. All the people fell upon their faces, crying out, 'The Lord, He is God! The Lord, He is God!' Elijah lost no time in striking a final blow against the idolaters. 'Take the prophets of Baal,' he exclaimed, 'let not one of them escape!' He was instantly obeyed and the false priests were slain to a man on the banks of the river Kishon.

The drought comes to an end

Elijah told Ahab, who seems to have been watching passively, that he could hear the sound of heavy rain. The king retired to his tent to eat and drink, whilst Elijah ascended Mount Carmel, and sat with his head bowed down between his knees. He sent his servant to look out over the sea for the first sign of rain in the west. Six times the lad reported that the sky was clear, and the prophet told him to look again; at the seventh he brought back the message, 'Behold there ariseth a cloud out of the sea, as small as a man's hand.' At this sign the prophet sent the king word to prepare his chariot and leave for his palace before the rain made the roads impassable. The heaven grew black with clouds, and Elijah ran through the torrential rain before the king's chariot, as a mark of homage, right up to the gates of Jezreel, a distance of about sixteen miles.

Elijah flees to Mount Horeb

When Ahab told Jezebel of Elijah's victory over the prophets of Baal, she vowed to put the prophet to death. Elijah was forced once again to escape her vengeance, and fled to Beer-sheba. From there he wandered about in the wilderness of Paran, until, overcome by fatigue and despair, he sat down under a juniper tree and prayed for death. 'O Lord,' he cried, 'take away my life, for I am no better than my fathers.' He fell asleep, but was awakened by an angel, and found beside him a loaf of bread and cruse (jar) of water. After he had refreshed himself, Elijah journeyed for another forty days and arrived at Mount Horeb. There, like Moses, he was favoured with a vision of God's glory. He heard God's voice asking, 'What doest thou here, Elijah?' In reply, the prophet complained that all his efforts had been in vain, for the children of Israel had forsaken God. Then Elijah witnessed in succession a terrible storm, an earthquake and a devastating fire, all symbols of God's power, followed by a still small voice which told him to continue his mission. In this way, Elijah was made to realize that the position was not as gloomy as he had thought. Justice and righteousness would yet be established, and Baal-worship destroyed. This would be accomplished by three people, whom Elijah was told to anoint. They were Hazael, the future king of Syria; Jehu, the son of Nimshi, as king of Israel; and Elisha, the son of Shaphat, to be Elijah's own successor. Elijah was also assured that there still remained a faithful minority of seven thousand, loyal to God. He realized his work had not been in vain, and that there was hope for the future.

Call of Elisha

Elijah immediately proceeded to carry out the third mission. Elisha lived in Abel-meholah, a place in the Jordan valley. He was ploughing with twelve yoke of oxen, guiding the twelfth himself, when Elijah arrived. Without saying a word, he cast his prophet's mantle on Elisha. Elisha only begged to be allowed to give his father and mother a parting embrace, and then followed his master.

Benhadad besieges Samaria

The last years of Ahab's reign were chiefly occupied by three great wars with Syria. Benhadad II, of Syria, led his army against the northern kingdom and besieged Samaria. He sent messengers to Ahab claiming all the king's possessions including his wives and children. Ahab was ready to submit, in the hope that Benhadad would be content with some token tribute. But the Syrian king now demanded that his soldiers ransack Ahab's palace and take away whatever they pleased. Courageously Ahab rejected this insulting demand and Benhadad declared that he would raze Samaria to the ground. Ahab replied with dignity, 'Let not him that girdeth on his armour boast as he that putteth it off'.

The king of Damascus received this message as he was carousing with his thirty-two confederate kings. At this juncture, a prophet came to tell Ahab that God had delivered the enemy into his hand. Ahab's small army of seven thousand men went out of the city, preceded by the two hundred and thirty-two young princes of the tribes. Benhadad who was drinking in his tent, contemptuously ordered them to be taken alive. But the princes and their followers rushed to the attack, the panic-stricken Syrians were pursued with great slaughter, and Benhadad barely escaped on his horse. The same prophet warned Ahab to expect a new attack in the following year.

The battle of Aphek

Benhadad's advisers now persuaded him to fight in the low country, for, they said, 'the god of Israel is a god of the hills'. So the Syrians advanced to Aphek, in the plain of Sharon. Again a prophet appeared to assure Ahab of complete victory. After facing each other for seven days, the armies joined battle and the Syrians were routed with a slaughter of one hundred thousand men. Moreover, the walls of the city of Aphek collapsed and buried twenty-seven thousand soldiers in the ruins. Benhadad took refuge inside Aphek and decided to throw himself on the mercy of Ahab, who foolishly welcomed him as his 'brother'. Ahab was content with Benhadad's promise to return the towns taken from Omri by Benhadad I (see page 107), and to grant him trading facilities in Damascus. For the fourth time in this war a prophet was sent to Ahab, this time to denounce him for his leniency, and to declare that God would take his life in place of the life of Benhadad.

Ahab covets Naboth's vineyard

Ahab's capital was Samaria, but his favourite residence was the beautiful city of Jezreel. Adjoining his palace was a vineyard owned by a man named Naboth. Ahab wished to acquire it as a vegetable garden and offered to buy it or exchange it for a better vineyard. Naboth refused as he did not wish to part with property inherited from his ancestors. Ahab behaved childishly by sulking and refusing to eat, but the wicked Jezebel solved his problem in her usual fashion. She wrote letters to the elders of Jezreel, in the king's name, to have Naboth put on trial on a false charge of blasphemy against God and the king. Two hired witnesses gave evidence and Naboth was found guilty and stoned to death. His vineyard was confiscated and passed into the possession of the crown. Elijah met Ahab at the vineyard and the king, conscience-stricken, called out, 'Hast thou found me, O mine enemy?' 'I have found thee,'

112

answered the prophet, and went on to denounce the king for his crime, 'In the place where the dogs licked the blood of Naboth shall dogs lick thy blood, even thine.' Jezebel's fate was to be still more terrible; the dogs would eat her under the walls of Jezreel and the whole house of Ahab would be wiped out. This was Elijah's last mission to Ahab, and he does not appear again till the next reign. For once, Ahab repented and humbled himself by fasting and wearing sackcloth.

The Assyrians launch an attack on Syria

In the spring of 853 B.C.E., Shalmaneser III of Assyria launched an attack on the neighbouring country of Syria, in an attempt to extend his boundaries westwards to the shores of the Mediterranean sea. A fierce battle was fought at Karkar in the north of Syria. An account is to be found on an Assyrian inscription which boasts of victory and claims the capture of two thousand chariots and the slaughter of ten thousand soldiers belonging to 'Ahab the Israelite'. It would seem therefore that there must have been a brief alliance between Israel and Syria against the common foe. In all probability the Assyrians retreated after the battle and hostilities were resumed between Ahab and Benhadad.

The prophet Micaiah issues a warning

Benhadad had refused to restore the cities of Israel, as he had promised (see page 112). Ahab took advantage of a visit from his ally, Jehoshaphat, whom he entertained, to propose a joint expedition for the recovery of Ramoth-gilead. The pious king of Judah agreed but wanted to consult God's prophets first. Ahab tried to satisfy him by summoning his own four hundred prophets who, with one voice, promised Ahab victory. Jehoshaphat asked if there were no more prophets and Ahab remembered a certain Micaiah, the son of Imlah, whom, however, he hated as he always predicted that evil would befall him. Micaiah was sent for and found the two kings upon their thrones, in their robes of state. One of the false prophets, Zedekiah the son of Chenaanah, had placed horns of iron on his head, to show how Ahab would push the Syrians to their destruction. Micaiah foretold the king's death by likening Israel to a flock without a shepherd, and denounced the other prophets as possessed by a lying spirit sent by God to deceive

Ahab. Upon this, Zedekiah struck and taunted him, and the king sent Micaiah to prison.

Ahab is killed in the battle of Ramoth-gilead

The words of Micaiah induced Ahab to disguise himself as a common soldier in the ensuing battle at Ramoth-gilead, while Jehoshaphat wore his own royal robes. Benhadad commanded his captains to direct all their force against the king of Israel. At first the enemy mistook Jehoshaphat for Ahab, but, on discovering their error, left him unharmed. In spite of his precautions, Ahab was mortally wounded by a chance shot from a bow which pierced his armour. He was supported in his chariot, while the battle raged, till sunset, and then he died. At the announcement of his death the cry went through the camp, 'Every man to his city, and every man to his country'. Ahab's body was brought to Samaria for burial, but not until the words spoken by Elijah at Naboth's vineyard were fulfilled. For as his chariot was washed out at the pool of Samaria, the dogs licked up his blood.

Jehoshaphat's reforms

Jehoshaphat returned to Jerusalem unharmed, but was rebuked by the prophet Jehu for allying himself with Ahab. The king now devoted himself with renewed zeal to the work of reformation. He went in person through his kingdom, from Beersheba to Mount Ephraim, bringing the people back to the God of their fathers. He appointed judges in all the fortified cities, and established a supreme court of appeal in Jerusalem. As we shall see in the next chapter, Jehoshaphat kept up his contacts with the northern kingdom, during the reigns of Ahaziah and Jehoram, Ahab's successors.

Jehoshaphat defeats the invaders of his territory

In the latter part of his reign, the Moabites, Ammonites and Edomites, on Judah's eastern frontier, invaded Jehoshaphat's territory. When the king heard that enemy hordes had reached Engedi on the western shore of the Dead Sea, he proclaimed a fast through all the land and, at an assembly before the Temple, offered up a prayer for Divine aid. The answer came in a striking and unusual form. The Spirit of God fell upon Jahaziel, a Levite of the family of Asaph, who assured the king that he would gain a victory without having to fight. The next morning Jehoshaphat and his army marched to the wilderness of Tekoa.

114

To their amazement they found a mass of corpses, for apparently the enemy had quarrelled among themselves and had fought a ferocious battle against each other. No less than three days were occupied in gathering the spoil, which was more than they could carry away, and on the fourth they assembled to renew their songs of praise in the valley which they called Berachah (blessing). This great deliverance struck terror into the hearts of all the nations, and peace reigned in Judah for the rest of Jehoshaphat's life.

Readings from the Bible

I Kings, chapter 18, verses 20 to 40   The challenge on Mount Carmel
I Kings, chapter 19, verses 1 to 18   Elijah at Mount Horeb
I Kings, chapter 21   Naboth's vineyard
II Chronicles, chapter 18, verses   Battle of Ramoth-gilead
     28 to 34

Exercises

1. List the main incidents in Elijah's prophetic career. Describe the part he played in opposing Jezebel's evil influence.
2. Give an account of Ahab's wars with Syria.
3. What incidents occurred at each of the following mountains? Mounts Sinai, Nebo, Tabor, Carmel and Gilboa.

17

THE HOUSE OF OMRI

Part II

AHAB was succeeded by his son Ahaziah, who, after a short reign of two years, was followed by his brother Jehoram, with whom Omri's dynasty came to an abrupt end. The outstanding figure during Jehoram's reign was the prophet Elisha, whose authority and influence altered the course of Israel's history. We shall now deal with this period in more detail.

The Reign of Ahaziah

Ahaziah is involved in two major disasters

Ahaziah, the eighth king of Israel, like his mother, was an ardent Baal worshipper. There are two short references in the Bible to his activities. He was associated with Jehoshaphat, king of Judah, in building a fleet of ships at Ezion-geber, on the Gulf of Akaba (as Solomon had done previously, see page 98), to bring gold from Ophir. The fleet was wrecked in a storm, and Jehoshaphat refused Ahaziah's proposal to join in a second venture. We also learn that Moab rebelled against Israel and refused to pay any further tribute. An attempt to quash the rebellion was made later by Jehoram (see page 118).

Elijah foretells Ahaziah's death

Ahaziah's reign was brief because he met with a serious accident when he fell from a lattice window in the upper room of his palace. The king sent messengers to the heathen shrine of Baal-zebub, in the Philistine city of Ekron, to enquire whether

116

he would recover from his injury. This brought Elijah again upon the scene. He met the king's messengers, denounced them for trying to consult an idol, and told them that their master would never leave his bed alive. The prophet was not personally known to the messengers, but from their description of him as 'a hairy man, girt with a girdle of leather about his loins', Ahaziah at once recognized Elijah the Tishbite, whose sharp words had been the terror of his father's court. He sent a captain with his band of fifty men to seize the prophet, who was living on Mount Carmel at the time. The captain called to him, 'Thou man of God, the king hath said, Come down'. 'If I be a man of God,' answered Elijah, 'let fire come down from heaven, and consume thee and thy fifty'. Immediately the captain and his men were destroyed by fire. A second captain of fifty went and repeated the order in a more commanding manner — 'Come down quickly' — but they suffered the same fate. The third implored Elijah to be merciful. The prophet accompanied him to the king's bedside and announced Ahaziah's approaching death. As Elijah had predicted, Ahaziah never rose again from his bed, but died, leaving his kingdom to his brother Jehoram.

Elijah ascends to heaven

The time had come for Elijah's work to be taken over by Elisha. Both prophets were at Gilgal, when Elijah received the Divine message that his end was near. Elisha persisted in following his master until the very last moment and accompanied him to Bethel. Some disciples of the prophets met Elisha with the words, 'Knowest thou that the Lord will take away thy master from thy head today?' He answered, 'I do know it, hold ye your peace'. The same scene was repeated at Jericho, and both arrived at the river Jordan, while a group of fifty prophets came out to gaze at them across the plain. Arriving at the river's edge, Elijah rolled up his sheepskin mantle and struck the water, which parted, and they went over to the other side on dry ground. Then they exchanged their last words. Elijah invited his successor to make his final request, and Elisha asked that a double portion of Elijah's spirit should rest upon him, so that he might prove worthy of his trust. 'Thou hast asked a hard thing,' said Elijah, 'nevertheless, if thou see me when I am taken from thee, it shall be so unto thee; but if not,

117

it shall not be so'. Suddenly, Elisha found himself separated from his master by a chariot and horses of fire, and Elijah was carried up by a whirlwind into heaven. Elisha saw him before he vanished in the sky, and, rending his clothes, cried out, 'My father! my father! The chariot of Israel, and the horsemen thereof!'

His request had been granted and Elisha took up the mantle which Elijah had let fall, and at once put his power to the proof by dividing the waters of Jordan on his return to Jericho, where the prophets, who had remained watching, welcomed him as Elijah's successor. In spite of Elisha's protest, the prophets sent fifty men in search of Elijah, thinking that God might have carried him away to some lonely mountain or valley. Their unsuccessful search lasted for three days.

Elisha purifies the bitter waters

While in Jericho, Elisha received a complaint from its citizens that they could not use the spring because the water was bitter. The prophet put salt in a new cruse and poured it into the spring, and the waters became drinkable. Elisha eventually made his home in Samaria.

The Reign of Jehoram of Israel

Jehoram marches against Mesha, king of Moab

Jehoram, the ninth king of Israel, was the son of Ahab and Jezebel, and the successor of his brother Ahaziah. He reigned for twelve years at Samaria. He was little better than his parents, for although he removed the images of Baal, perhaps due to Elisha's influence, he still tolerated the idolatrous worship established by Jeroboam I.

Early in his reign, he sent an expeditionary force against Mesha, the rebellious king of the Moabites, who refused to pay his annual tribute of wool shorn from one hundred thousand lambs and one hundred thousand rams. Jehoram found a ready ally in Jehosphaphat, who himself had previously repelled an attack by the forces of Moab, Ammon and Edom against the kingdom of Judah (see page 114). It was decided that the united forces should march round the Dead Sea and invade Moab from the south. On this occasion they received the support of the king of Edom, who had evidently severed his former alliance with Moab.

118

After a seven days' march through the desert region, the armies were without water and were in danger of dying of thirst. Jehoram was convinced that disaster was inevitable. The pious Jehoshaphat, however, proposed that a true prophet be consulted, and it was found that Elisha was in the camp. The three kings approached him, and Elisha, out of consideration for Jehoshaphat, agreed to prophesy coming events. Bidding them dig trenches all over the valley, he promised that God would give them not only water, but a complete victory over Moab. In the night the trenches were dug, and in the morning, water flowed into them from the hills of Edom. The reflection of the rising sun's rays in the water deceived the Moabites into thinking that the plain was covered with blood and that the allies had destroyed each other. Raising the cry, 'Now, therefore, Moab, to the spoil,' they rushed upon the camp, were met by the allied armies and were pursued into their own country with immense slaughter.

This victory was followed up by an exterminating war. The cities of Moab were destroyed, the fields filled with stones, the springs stopped up, and the fruit-trees cut down. The only city left was the fortress of Kir-haraseth. Even this was on the point of being taken by storm, when the king of Moab, with seven hundred warriors, tried to cut his way through to reach the king of Edom who, he still hoped, might come to his aid. The attempt failed and, in desperation, Mesha mounted the wall in sight of the besiegers, and offered his eldest son and heir as a burnt-offering to Moloch. Horrified at the sight, the allied troops retreated and returned to their own countries.

The Moabite stone The biblical account of the Moabite revolt against Omri and his successors is strikingly confirmed by the inscription on the monument known as the Moabite Stone or Stone of Mesha. Written in the Phoenician script used by the Hebrews of the period, it was discovered in the year 1868 on the site of Dibon, the Moabite capital, and now stands in the Louvre, in Paris. On it, Mesha, king of Moab, relates how Omri of Israel had afflicted Moab for many years because Chemosh, god of the Moabites, was angry. Omri's son (Ahab), had also said he would afflict Moab. 'And Omri possessed the land of Medeba . . . and Chemosh restored it in my days.' Mesha claims not

119

only to have driven out the invaders but to have annexed enemy territory. No mention is made of the withdrawal of Jehoram's and Jehoshaphat's troops for the reason mentioned above. This is not surprising since, in most of the ancient monuments so far discovered, the kings boast of their successes and ignore their failures.

Elisha performs several miraculous acts

During Jehoram's reign, Elisha became known as a saintly man of God. In this section, we shall give an account of six incidents in his career which illustrate his readiness to assist those in need.

The miracle of the widow's oil

(i) On one occasion, he listened sympathetically to the appeal for help from a poor widow, whose husband had been a member of the prophetic guild, and who had died in debt. The creditor had claimed her two sons in payment and intended to sell them as slaves. When Elisha heard that all she possessed was a pot of oil, he told her to borrow as many vessels as possible and pour the oil into them. Miraculously, she was able to fill all the vessels, and having sold the oil, not only paid her debt, but had sufficient money left over to maintain herself and her sons.

The Shunammite woman is rewarded for her hospitality

(ii) During his frequent travels, Elisha often stopped at the small village of Shunem to enjoy a meal as a guest of a certain wealthy and hospitable woman. With her husband's consent, she had a special guest-room built for the prophet on the roof of their house so that he could stay there whenever he wished. During one of his visits, Elisha told his servant Gehazi that he would like to see his hostess. He asked whether he could repay her hospitality by using his influence with the king or military authorities to protect her estate, if the need arose. The woman replied that this was unnecessary as her relatives, among whom she dwelt, were sufficient guarantee against injustice. On hearing from Gehazi that she was childless, Elisha told her that a son would be born to her in the following year.

The prophet's words were fulfilled but a few years later while the boy was in the fields with his father during the harvest he was suddenly affected by the heat, collapsed and died. The grief-stricken mother laid the child on the prophet's bed, and immediately set out for Mount Carmel, where Elisha was staying. Seeing her approaching, Elisha sent Gehazi to meet her and enquire whether all was well. She replied briefly, 'It is well', and hurried on. As soon as she reached Elisha, she poured out her heart. The prophet sent Gehazi to Shunem with his staff to lay it on the child's face, but the mother refused to leave Elisha until he went back with her. As they approached the house, Gehazi met them with the news that the child was still dead. The prophet then went up to his room and uttered a silent prayer. He stretched himself over the child's body and gradually it began to show signs of life and opened its eyes. The Shunammite woman was called, and after bowing gratefully to the prophet carried her son away in her arms.

Some time later, the Shunammite woman was forced to leave her city because of famine, and stayed among the Philistines for seven years. On her return she found that her land had been taken away from her. She appealed to Jehoram for justice at the very moment when Gehazi was telling the king how the prophet had restored her child to life. Jehoram immediately gave orders for her land to be restored together with the value of its produce during the previous seven years.

The poisonous pottage is made harmless

(iii) At Gilgal, during a famine, Elisha sat down to a meal with a group of prophets. By mistake, one of them threw some wild gourds and grapes into the pot. When they tasted the pottage they realized it was poisonous, but Elisha told them to throw some meal into the pot and the dish was rendered harmless.

Twenty loaves suffice for one hundred men

(iv) A man arrived at Gilgal from Baal-shalishah, bringing Elisha a first-fruit offering of twenty loaves of barley and some fresh ears of corn. Elisha told his servant to distribute the food amongst the hundred men in his company. In spite of the servant's protest that there was insufficient for so many, the prophet assured him that not only would there be enough but some would be left over. This proved to be the case.

The axe-head is recovered

(v) Some prophets decided to build a new settlement in the valley of the Jordan. As they were felling trees for this purpose, the head of a borrowed axe flew off and sunk in the water.

Elisha told the man who had lost it to show him the exact place where the axe had fallen. He then threw a stick into the stream, and the iron head floated to the surface.

Naaman is cured of his leprosy

(vi) Elisha's fame had reached the country of Syria, where Naaman, a captain of the army, was afflicted with leprosy. One of his wife's servants was a captive Israelite maid who told her mistress that if only Naaman would consult Elisha, he could be healed. When Naaman heard of this, he spoke to his king, Benhadad, who immediately wrote a letter to Jehoram, the king of Israel, requesting him to bring about a cure. The captain duly arrived at Samaria, bringing valuable gifts, and presented the letter in person to Jehoram, who could only conclude that Benhadad was picking a quarrel with him. Elisha heard of the king's worries and asked for Naaman to be sent to his house. Naaman arrived with his horses and chariots, and received a message from Elisha to bathe in the river Jordan seven times, after which he would be cured. Naaman was indignant; why should he bathe in the Jordan when the native rivers of Amanah and Pharpar were much better? He turned away in rage, but his servants persuaded him to carry out such a simple request. Naaman dipped himself seven times in the river Jordan and was completely cured of his leprosy. Gratefully he returned to Elisha's house and offered him a gift which the prophet refused. Naaman thereupon asked to be given two mules' burden of soil to take back with him, with which to build an altar to God, who had restored him to health. He acknowledged God's supremacy and asked to be forgiven if he had to accompany his master to the temple of the god Rimmon.

Elisha's servant, Gehazi, who had been present, saw an opportunity to enrich himself. He ran after Naaman and invented a story that two young members of the prophetic guild had arrived to see Elisha. The prophet would appreciate a gift of a talent of silver and two changes of raiment, on their behalf. Naaman willingly gave twice the amount to Gehazi, who hid the silver and clothes in his room. On his returning to his master's presence, he denied that he had been anywhere, but Elisha was well aware of his dishonesty. His punishment was severe, for Gehazi was afflicted with the disease of leprosy from which Naaman had just been cured.

122

The Syrians began to plan a campaign against the Northern Kingdom, and often sent guerrilla bands across the border. Elisha kept King Jehoram informed of the enemy's plans and movements and so saved him from being captured. Benhadad at first suspected treachery among his own officers, but soon learned of Elisha's remarkable powers. He therefore sent a force to Dothan, ten miles north of Samaria, to capture the prophet who was living there. The army besieged the city but, at Elisha's prayer, the Syrian forces were struck with blindness and Elisha himself led them to Samaria. When their sight was restored, they were astonished to find themselves captives. Jehoram wished to have them executed but Elisha directed him to give them food and return them to their native land.

*Benhadad's troops
besiege Samaria*

Benhadad was now determined to capture Samaria and his huge army besieged the city. Before long, the citizens suffered from severe famine to such an extent that mothers were even killing their children for food. When Jehoram heard this he was filled with horror and put on sackcloth as a sign of mourning. He blamed Elisha for the calamity and sent a messenger to take the prophet's life. When the messenger arrived at Elisha's house he was held back by the prophet's friends. Suddenly the king himself arrived and Elisha told him that on the very next day there would be ample food in the city. One of the captains, who had accompanied the king, mocked him for making such a stupid statement. Elisha replied that the captain would see the miracle with his own eyes but would not eat a morsel of food.

*The story of the
four lepers*

There was a leper colony outside the city, and four starving lepers decided to surrender to the enemy, as they had little to lose. On entering the camp they found that the Syrians had fled, for alarmed by the mysterious sound of an advancing army, they thought that the Hittites and Egyptians had been hired to come to Jehoram's aid. The lepers ate their fill, and hid some silver and gold and clothes. Realizing they would be punished if they concealed the joyful news, they told the keeper of the city-gate all that had happened. Jehoram arose in the middle of the night and sent some soldiers to discover whether the story

123

was true. They found heaps of garments and vessels which the Syrians had thrown away in their haste. When the news spread in the city, the citizens rushed out, appeased their hunger, and food became plentiful. The captain who had mocked Elisha was placed in charge of the main gate, and was trampled to death in the rush. Thus Elisha's prophecy was fulfilled.

The Reign of Jehoram of Judah

The cruel and unpopular Jehoram nearly loses his kingdom

If you glance at the chart on page 106, you will find that during the period described above, another Jehoram was on the throne of the southern kingdom. He had succeeded his father Jehoshaphat as the fifth king of Judah, about the year 849 B.C.E., and reigned for seven years. Through his ill-fated marriage with Athaliah, the daughter of Ahab and Jezebel, he followed the idolatrous practices of that evil family. As soon as he ascended the throne, he displayed the utmost cruelty by having all his brothers murdered. He was an unpopular king and his reign proved disastrous. The Edomites revolted and secured their independence, and his kingdom was nearly overthrown by an invasion of the Philistines and Arabians who had been tributary to his father. They stormed and plundered the king's palace and carried off his wives and children except his youngest son Ahaziah. Jehoram suffered from an incurable disease, from which he died, and was succeeded by Ahaziah, the sixth king of Judah, who was destined to reign only one year.

As we shall see in the next chapter, both Ahaziah of Judah and Jehoram of Israel met their death during the revolt of Jehu, who founded a new dynasty.

———————⟶•⟵———————

Readings from the Bible

II Kings, chapter 2, verses 1 to 18   Elijah's ascent to heaven
II Kings, chapter 4, verses 8 to 37   The Shunammite woman
II Kings, chapter 5   The story of Naaman
II Kings, chapter 7, verses 3 to 20   The relief of Samaria

Exercises

1. Give an account of Jehoshaphat's alliances with Ahab, Ahaziah, and Jehoram (see pages 113, 116 and 118).
2. Compare the characters of Elijah and Elisha.
3. Write briefly on the following:
   (a) Ahaziah of Israel; (b) the Shunammite woman; (c) the Moabite stone; (d) Naaman.

124

18

THE HOUSE OF JEHU

Part I

Kings of Judah	Approximate dates of accession, B.C.E.	Kings of Israel	Approximate dates of accession, B.C.E.
(Athaliah)	841	Jehu	841
Joash	835	Jehoahaz	814
Amaziah	797	Jehoash	798
Uzziah	790	Jeroboam II	784
		Zechariah	743

Benhadad is murdered by Hazael

THE time had arrived for the fulfilment of the divine assurance given to Elijah some fifteen years previously (see page 111), that Baal worship would be utterly destroyed. Of the three commissions entrusted to Elijah (see page 111), only one, the appointment of Elisha as his successor, had actually been carried out. It was left to Elisha to complete the task. After the Syrian flight from Samaria (see page 123), Benhadad returned to his capital, Damascus, and, before long, became very ill. This was the moment Elisha chose for visiting the city. Benhadad heard of his arrival and sent Hazael, one of his chief military officers, with gifts to enquire of the man of God whether he would recover. The reply was puzzling — the king could recover, but would surely die. Hazael, who obviously had designs on the throne, stared intently at the prophet, who burst into tears. Hazael asked the reason for such emotion, and Elisha foretold the cruelties he would inflict on the children of Israel, once he became king of Syria. History provides many examples where ambition has plunged men into crime. Hazael was no exception. He returned to Benhadad, assured him he would recover, and the very next day suffocated the king with a damp cloth, and seized the throne.

The Reign of Jehu

Jehu is proclaimed king of Israel

About this time, Jehoram of Israel, with Ahaziah of Judah as his ally, attempted to recapture Ramoth-gilead, the scene of Ahab's death. Jehoram, wounded in a battle with the Syrians, returned to Jezreel for medical attention, and Ahaziah went to visit him shortly afterwards. During their absence from the battle-front, Elisha sent one of his disciples to Ramoth-gilead to anoint Jehu, son of Jehoshaphat, the son of Nimshi, one of the chief captains, king of Israel. Calling Jehu to leave his brother officers, the prophet took him into an inner room, anointed him king, and charged him to destroy utterly the house of Ahab and avenge the murdered prophets. Jehu returned to his comrades and, urged on by them, revealed the secret of the prophet's mission. This was the signal for revolt. The captains spread out their cloaks on the top of the stairs to form a 'royal' carpet for Jehu to stand on, blew the trumpets, and shouted 'Jehu is king'.

Jehoram is killed, and Ahaziah dies of his wounds

Everything now depended on speed. After taking precautions to prevent anyone leaving Ramoth-gilead to spread the news, Jehu mounted his chariot and drove straight to Jezreel. The approach of his party was announced by the watchman on the city tower, and Jehoram, anxious to know how the war was going, sent a horseman to meet him. To the question, 'Is it peace?' Jehu answered, 'What has thou to do with peace? Turn behind me!' A second messenger was sent to meet Jehu, with the same result. By this time they were near enough for the watchman to recognize Jehu by his furious driving. Jehoram mounted his chariot, and went out with Ahaziah to meet Jehu at a fateful spot, the field of Naboth the Jezreelite. Jehoram, who still thought that Jehu had come with news of the war asked, 'Is it peace?' 'What peace,' retorted Jehu, 'so long as the harlotries of your mother Jezebel and her witchcrafts are so many?' Crying to Ahaziah, 'There is treachery', Jehoram fled,

126

but an arrow from Jehu's bow pierced his heart, and he fell dead in his chariot. Then Jehu told Bidkar, his adjutant, to throw the corpse into the field of Naboth, which Ahab had once seized. Ahaziah was pursued by Jehu's soldiers and was severely wounded when he reached a place called Ibleam, about eight miles south of Jezreel, but he managed to reach Megiddo, where he died. His body was taken by his servants to Jerusalem and buried there.

Death of Jezebel

Jehu now rushed to the royal palace to execute vengeance on Jezebel. In spite of her wickedness, the queen was no coward. In her royal headdress, and with painted eyebrows, she looked down defiantly from the latticed window of her palace on the city wall, and saluted Jehu as a second 'Zimri' (see page 106). But she, too, had traitors in her palace, and, at the call of Jehu, some of her attendants threw her down into the courtyard. Her blood spattered the city wall, and Jehu drove his chariot over her mangled corpse. It was not until Jehu had sat down to eat that he gave the command, 'See now to this cursed woman and bury her, for she is a king's daughter.' They went and found that the dogs had devoured her flesh, fulfilling the words of Elijah (see page 113).

Jehu destroys the house of Ahab and puts an end to Baal-worship

There were still seventy sons of Ahab left in Samaria. Jehu wrote letters to the elders, mockingly challenging them to elect the best man king and decide the succession on the battlefield. Terrified, they replied that they fully submitted to his will. A second letter ordered them to bring him the heads of all the seventy to Jezreel on the very next day, and this brutal order was carried out immediately. All that remained of Ahab's family in Jezreel were hunted down and slaughtered, together with their supporters. On his way to Samaria, Jehu met forty-two relatives of Ahaziah, journeying to Jezreel to pay their respects to the royal family. Obviously they did not know what had happened. At Jehu's order they were seized and killed, and their bodies were thrown into the well of a nearby shearing house.

Jehu also met Jehonadab, the son of Rechab, afterwards famous as the founder of a religious order called the Rechabites, who had opposed Baal worship. Jehu invited Jehonadab to mount his chariot and witness his zeal for the Lord. Arriving at Samaria, Jehu devised a cunning plan to destroy all Baal worship at one stroke. Declaring that 'Ahab served Baal a little, but Jehu will serve him much', he proclaimed a solemn assembly for Baal in the temple which Ahab had built at Samaria. The Baal worshippers arrived from all parts of the kingdom and, at Jehu's request, wore the special robes kept for such occasions. Jehu and Jehonadab entered the temple. As soon as Jehu had offered a sacrifice, he gave the signal to eighty armed men, stationed at the gates. They rushed in and butchered the worshippers to the last man. The huge stone statue of Baal was broken in pieces, the other images were burned, and the temple razed to the ground. Jehu thus became the tenth king of Israel, and reigned for twenty-eight years.

Although Jehu banned Baal worship, he allowed the heathen shrines at Dan and Bethel to continue. This was probably a political move since Jehu did not wish his subjects to be attracted to the temple in Jerusalem in the kingdom of Judah.

Jehu pays tribute to Shalmaneser of Assyria

In the year 841 B.C.E., soon after Jehu's accession, Shalmaneser III of Assyria again launched an attack on Syria (see page 113). His army defeated Hazael's forces and besieged Damascus. Then Shalmaneser pressed southward and exacted tributes from the Phoenicians and from Jehu, king of Israel. We learn all this from the 'Black Obelisk', discovered in 1845, on which the Assyrian emperor records his successes in pictorial form. One of the portraits shows Jehu paying homage to the conqueror, and the caption reads, 'The tribute of Jehu, son of Omri. I received from him silver, gold, golden goblets . . . and javelins.' Shalmaneser was forced to withdraw because of threats to his own empire by neighbouring countries. Hazael immediately invaded Israel's territory in Transjordan, and Jehu was too weak to offer any resistance.

The Reign of Jehoahaz

Jehu was succeeded by his son Jehoahaz, the eleventh king of Israel, who reigned for seventeen years in Samaria. During this period, Hazael completed his conquest of the northern kingdom, and Jehoahaz was humiliated to such an extent that

128

he was allowed to maintain a force of only ten thousand infantry, fifty horsemen and ten chariots.

Athaliah seizes the throne of Judah

We now return to the history of the southern kingdom, during the years 841 to 798 B.C.E., when Jehu and Jehoahaz ruled over the kingdom of Israel. After Ahaziah's death (see page 127), Athaliah, the queen-mother, and the last member of Ahab's house, seized the throne and immediately had all the members of the royal household killed. She was unaware, however, that Joash, Ahaziah's infant son, was still alive, for he had been hidden in the Temple buildings by his aunt Jehosheba, the wife of the high-priest Jehoiada. In spite of all the wicked queen's efforts to force Baal-worship on the people, the majority completely ignored her and remained faithful to God. In the seventh year of Athaliah's reign, Jehoiada decided the moment was ripe to put an end to her tyranny and place the real heir on the throne. Obtaining the support of five military leaders, he showed them the young prince, and they organized a meeting of the Levites and civic heads in the Temple, where they all took an oath of allegiance.

Joash is anointed king

To avoid any suspicion, the *coup d'état* (the overthrow of a government by force) was arranged on a Sabbath day, when it was the normal practice for the priests and Levites to enter the Temple to organize their duties for the coming week. They divided themselves into three sections, each guarding one of the main entrances. The captains with their men, armed with spears and shields, took up their stations to prevent anyone entering, while the courtyard outside was filled with people. When everything was ready, Joash was brought into the Temple. Jehoiada anointed him, and the people shouted, 'Long live the king'.

The shouting of the people reached the ears of the queen-mother, who, hastening from her place to the Temple, found her grandson standing on the raised platform, while the trumpets sounded and the people rejoiced. She tore her clothes and cried out, 'Treason, treason'. Jehoiada ordered the captains to take her out of the sacred enclosure, and they killed her at the entrance of 'the horse-gate' by the royal palace. The people and king took a solemn oath that they would be faithful to God, the temple of Baal was destroyed with all the idols,

129

and the false priest Mattan was slain before his own altar. Then the young king was brought in procession to the royal palace, 'so all the people of the land rejoiced, and the city was quiet'.

The Reign of Joash

Joash repairs the Temple

Joash, the seventh king of Judah, was only seven years old when he ascended the throne. During the first twenty-three years of his reign under the guidance of the high-priest Jehoiada, 'he did that which was right in the Lord's eyes'. One of his pious acts was to repair and purify the Temple, which had been plundered and damaged during Athaliah's reign. At first, Joash ordered the expenses to be met from the people's offerings, but this method proved too slow. Joash scolded the priests for the delay in completing the repairs and told them to stop this form of collection. Instead, the people put their offerings into a chest, placed near the altar by Jehoiada. It was emptied at intervals and the money handed direct to the supervisors in charge of the project. Before long the repairs were completed, and there was even enough money left over to provide vessels for the Sanctuary.

The king changes his policy, and Judah is invaded

Jehoiada, the high-priest, died at the age of one hundred and thirty, and was buried in the royal tombs, as a tribute to his outstanding services. Then came an immediate change in the king's policy and character. The princes of Judah, who had probably been jealous of the high priest's influence, persuaded the king that it was time for him to be his own master. This resulted in the neglect of God's house and a revival of idol worship. Zechariah, the son of Jehoiada, who warned Joash of the consequences, was stoned to death in the Temple court by the king's command.

The last years of Joash proved calamitous. Hazael, the king of Syria, had overrun the Transjordan provinces of Israel during the reign of Jehoahaz (see page 128). After a campaign against the Philistines, he marched towards Jerusalem where his small force defeated the whole army of Judah. Jerusalem itself was only saved from the horrors of a massacre by the surrender of all the holy vessels and treasures, both in the Temple and the king's palace. Scarcely had the Syrians with-

130

drawn when Joash became seriously ill, and was assassinated in his bed by two of his servants. He was succeeded by his son Amaziah.

———————⟶•⊏——————

Readings from the Bible

II Kings, chapter 9   Jehu's rebellion
II Kings, chapter 12   Joash repairs the Temple

Exercises

1. Explain how the three commissions entrusted to Elijah (see page 111) were carried out. What were their results?
2. How were Elijah's prophecies about Ahab and Jezebel fulfilled?
3. Jehu has been described as 'a brave soldier, but secretive and cruel'. Mention incidents in Jehu's career to show whether you agree or disagree with this statement.
4. Give an account of the reign of Joash.

19

THE HOUSE OF JEHU

Part II

The Reigns of Jehoash of Israel and Amaziah of Judah

BOTH Jehoash and Amaziah ascended the throne within a few months of each other. During the early part of their reigns, each was occupied in recovering territory previously captured by their enemies. Later, as we shall see, Amaziah launched an unsuccessful attack against Jehoash.

Jehoash visits Elisha on his death-bed

Jehoash, the twelfth king of Israel, reigned for sixteen years. Although, like his predecessors, he maintained pagan shrines, his character was not altogether bad. He seems to have had a great affection for the prophet Elisha, now an old man. Elisha was seriously ill, and the king wept over him, on his death-bed. The Syrians were still the greatest menace to Israel's safety, but they were beginning to loosen their hold owing to repeated campaigns by the Assyrians against them. Jehoash was naturally anxious to learn from the prophet whether the time was opportune to throw off the Syrian yoke. Elisha told the king to shoot an arrow from the open window in the direction of Damascus, whilst he himself laid his hands, together with the king's, upon the bow as if to give divine power to the shot. Jehoash was assured that he would defeat the Syrians at Aphek. Then, at the prophet's request, the king took the remaining arrows and hit the ground with them, but did so three times only. The prophet was angry with him for not continuing, as this meant that his victories would be limited to three. Soon after, Elisha died and was deeply mourned. Jehoash launched three successful campaigns against the enemy and regained all the cities Hazael had taken from his father.

Amaziah defeats the Edomites

Meanwhile, Amaziah, the eighth king of Judah, was similarly occupied. After ordering his father's murderers to be executed, he prepared an expedition for the recovery of Edom, which had revolted against his great-grandfather Jehoram (see page 124). Edom, too, had been attacked by Assyria, and its military strength had been considerably weakened. Amaziah increased his considerable force of three hundred thousand soldiers by hiring an additional one hundred thousand picked men of Israel. He dismissed them, however, when warned by a prophet that 'the Lord was not with Israel', and if he employed them defeat would follow. In anger, the mercenaries returned home but, on their way, sacked several Judaean cities. Amaziah advanced into 'the valley of salt', south of the Dead Sea, defeated the Edomites with great loss, and captured the rocky fortress of Sela. Surprisingly, the king brought the Edomite idols to Jerusalem and worshipped them. Because of this, a prophet foretold his ultimate destruction.

Amaziah challenges Jehoash of Israel

Flushed with victory, and probably provoked by the conduct of the Israelite mercenaries, Amaziah declared war on Jehoash. The king of Israel replied with a parable, in which he compared Amaziah to the thistle in Mount Lebanon demanding the daughter of the cedar in marriage, when a wild beast trod on it and crushed it. The king of Judah, said Jehoash, should not boast because he had defeated Edom, but stay quietly at home, lest he and his domain perish together. Amaziah ignored the warning and the armies met at Beth-shemesh, in Judaean territory. Jehoash inflicted a heavy defeat on Amaziah, and led him in triumph, as prisoner, to Jerusalem. He then broke down sections of Jerusalem's walls, ransacked the Temple and palace of their treasures, and returned to Samaria with hostages. Jehoash died soon after and was succeeded by his son, Jeroboam II.

Amaziah had been allowed to retain his throne but no longer

held his people's confidence and loyalty. Some years later the leaders rebelled, and he fled to Lachish, but was overtaken and assassinated. His son, Uzziah, succeeded him.

The Reigns of Jeroboam II of Israel and Uzziah of Judah

The kingdoms of Israel and Judah enjoy great prosperity

During the reigns of Jeroboam II in Israel and Uzziah in Judah, both kingdoms enjoyed the greatest prosperity in their history. No longer menaced by Syria (see page 132), their military gains ensured a long period of peace and stability. Jeroboam II, the thirteenth king of Israel, reigned for forty-one years at Samaria. Not only did he recapture from the Syrians the Trans Jordanic province of Gilead (see page 130), but subdued the Moabites and Ammonites, who became tributary to him.

Uzziah, the ninth king of Judah, was only sixteen years old when he succeeded his father, and reigned for fifty-two years. He was one of the ablest kings of Judah, serving God and enjoying unbroken prosperity. Uzziah's military successes were numerous. With his powerful army he regained the famous port of Elath, and subdued the Philistines and Arabians, former enemies of Judah (see page 124). He also repaired the wall of Jerusalem, which had been broken down after his father's defeat by Jehoash (see page 133), and skilful experts invented ballistic machines which were placed at strategic points of the city's fortifications. Uzziah was very fond of farming and encouraged his subjects to take an interest in agriculture. Wells were dug in the maritime plain (the Shephelah) for the king's numerous flocks, and farmers were employed to look after the royal estates.

Uzziah is punished for his arrogance

Unfortunately, Uzziah's success caused his downfall. Later in his reign he became so arrogant that he assumed the priestly functions and entered the Holy Place to burn incense on the golden altar. He was followed by the high-priest Azariah, accompanied by eighty courageous priests, prepared to prevent the violation of God's laws by force, if necessary. Azariah reproved the king and warned him to leave the sanctuary. Uzziah fell into a rage and suddenly, as he stood, censer in hand, a spot of leprosy broke out on his forehead. The king hastened

134

from the sanctuary and remained a leper to the day of his death. He was forced to live in isolation, and his son Jotham was appointed to act as regent in his place. When Uzziah died, he was not buried in the royal tomb but in a neighbouring field.

The voice of the Prophets

To judge by their military successes the future of both kingdoms appeared, on the surface, to be extremely bright. But there was a darker side to the picture. In their writings the prophets Amos and Hosea provide an insight into the internal life of the northern kingdom, and describe a society which was morally and religiously corrupt. The prophet Isaiah, who received his call in the year of Uzziah's death, was destined to play a major part in Judah's history (see page 147).

Amos prophesied during the latter part of Jeroboam's reign. Hosea commenced his prophecies about the same time but continued after the king's death during the reigns of his immediate successors. We shall therefore summarize Hosea's message in the next chapter.

The life and prophecies of Amos

Amos is the first of the 'literary' prophets, i.e., those whose prophecies have been preserved in written form. He was a simple countryman earning a living as a herdsman or shepherd in the small town of Tekoa, about twelve miles south of Jerusalem, and was also employed in the cultivation of sycamore trees. He received the divine call to deliver his message during the reigns of Uzziah of Judah and of Jeroboam II of Israel. About the year 765 B.C.E., he left his flocks and journed northwards to the kingdom of Israel to preach his message. At Bethel, the main national sanctuary, he uttered his stern warnings and rebukes to the worshippers.

What reasons impelled the prophet to do so? The answers can be stated simply. Untold luxury and prosperity had corrupted the rich to such an extent that they had lost all sense of justice and righteousness. Furthermore, although the shrines were crowded with people, the pure worship of God had been replaced by paganism. No nation, the prophet declared, would escape punishment for its sins. God ruled over the entire universe, and Syria, Philistia, Tyre, Edom, Ammon and Moab, all faced inevitable destruction for their sinful conduct. Nor should Judah or Israel lull themselves into thinking they would escape because they had been specially chosen as God's people.

The prophet attacks the idle rich for oppressing the poor

Amos was especially enraged at the oppression of the poor by the rich. In Samaria, the wealthy citizens, urged on by their wives, built summer and winter houses, with costly panels made of ivory. They lay stretched out on their ivory couches, wining and dining, without a care in the world. All this wealth was acquired by trampling on the poor. Cruel creditors charged excessive interest, and when their debtors could not pay, they sold them into slavery. There was not a law court in the land where they could ask for justice. God, proclaimed the prophet, despised the hypocrites, who brought sacrifices, when their personal lives were so evil. They defrauded the poor, falsified measures and scales, and cheated the innocent. In consequence of such evil, Israel would be overthrown and its people taken captive into a foreign land.

Amaziah tells Amos to return home

While Amos was in Bethel, Amaziah, the local priest, informed Jeroboam that the prophet was conspiring against the throne, and advised Amos to return to Judah and prophesy there. Threats did not worry Amos, and he foretold that severe punishment would overtake Amaziah and his family when the enemy attacked. Only through a change of heart could punishment be averted.

'Seek good, and not evil, that ye may live.
And so the Lord, the God of hosts, shall be with you,
    as ye have spoken.
Hate the evil, and love the good, and establish justice
    in the gate.
It may be that the Lord, God of hosts, will be gracious
    unto the remnant of Joseph.'

Amos ended his prophecies with a message of hope. The day would come when the people would return to their land, and the dynasty of David be restored to its former splendour.

The end of Jehu's dynasty

Jehu's dynasty ended in tragedy. Jeroboam II was succeeded by his son, Zechariah, the fourteenth king of Israel. After a short reign of six months, he was assassinated by the rebel leader, Shallum, the son of Jabesh. Within a generation of

136

Jeroboam's death, Amos' prophecies were fulfilled. Rebellion after rebellion followed, until the northern kingdom vanished from the pages of history.

———————➤•⟵———————

Readings from
the Bible

II Kings, chapter 14, verses 9 and 10   Jehoash's parable
II Kings, chapter 14, verses 23 to 29   Jeroboam II
Amos, chapter 6, verses 1 to 8   Amos denounces the nobles
Amos, chapter 7, verses 10 to 17   Amaziah accuses Amos

Exercises

1. Explain Jehoash's parable in more detail. What was its application?
2. In whose reign did Amos live? Give a brief account of his prophecies.
3. Amos is one of the twelve 'minor prophets'. What does the term 'minor prophet' mean? Mention as many of the others as you can.
4. Write briefly on the following:
   (*a*) Hazael; (*b*) Uzziah; (*c*) Amaziah, priest of Bethel.

20

DECLINE AND FALL OF THE NORTHERN KINGDOM

	Approximate dates			Approximate dates
Kings of Judah	of accession, B.C.E.		Kings of Israel	of accession, B.C.E.
Jotham			Shallum	742
(co-regent with				
Uzziah)	c. 751			
(ascended the throne)	740			
			Menahem	742
			Pekahiah	737
			Pekah	736
Ahaz	735			
			Hoshea	731

The Assyrian menace

THE treacherous Shallum, the fifteenth king of Israel, retained the throne for only one month, when he, in his turn, was overthrown and put to death by another conspirator, Menahem the son of Gadi. Menahem, the sixteenth king of Israel, who had seized the former capital of Tirzah as soon as Jeroboam died, was a barbaric ruler. He massacred the entire population of a city which had opposed him.

The kingdom was torn with internal strife, and stood little chance of withstanding the attack which came from mighty Assyria. In the year 745 B.C.E., Tiglath-pileser III, called 'Pul' in the Bible, seized the Assyrian throne after a revolt. The Assyrians had previously made attacks on Syria and Israel from time to time (see pages 113 and 132), but were unable to consolidate their gains because of domestic disturbances, and were

138

forced to retreat. Within a few years after his accession, Tiglath-pileser, having crushed all opposition, marched westward to conquer the lands beyond the Euphrates. In this way, he planned to gain access to the Mediterranean and to Egypt. Menahem was in no position to resist, and placed himself at the mercy of the Assyrian king, hoping thereby to retain his tottering throne. Tiglath-pileser agreed not to occupy Israel in return for a payment of one thousand talents of silver. This event is confirmed by an Assyrian inscription, which relates how Pul overwhelmed Menahem and imposed a heavy tribute on him. Menahem was succeeded by his son, Pekahiah, the seventeenth king of Israel, who was assassinated within two years of his accession by Pekah, the son of Remaliah, a leader of the anti-Assyrian movement.

The Reigns of Jotham and Ahaz

The Syrian-Israelite coalition ends in disaster

While these violent events were taking place in the northern kingdom, Jotham had succeeded his father, Uzziah, as the tenth king of Judah. On the whole, he was a pious king, who applied himself energetically to strengthening his country's defences. Across the border, Pekah, the eighteenth king of Israel, formed an alliance with Rezin, king of Syria, for the purpose of attacking Assyria. It would obviously be to their advantage if Jotham joined them, but the king of Judah wisely did not wish to be involved and refused their request. Pekah and Rezin were about to march against the southern kingdom when Jotham died; he was succeeded by his son, Ahaz, the eleventh king of Judah.

Ahaz, too, refused to join the coalition. The two kings at once invaded Judah and besieged Jerusalem, intending to replace Ahaz by a puppet of their own choice. Simultaneously, and most probably by previous arrangement, the Edomites marched on Judah from the south, while the Philistines raided border towns in the Negeb and Shephelah. Ahaz, against the prophet Isaiah's advice (see page 148), appealed to Tiglath-pileser for help, and sent him valuable gifts from the Temple and royal treasures. The Assyrian king responded immediately and began, as we learn from his inscriptions, by defeating the Philistines in the year 734 B.C.E. Within two years the districts of Galilee and Gilead had been captured from Israel, Damascus besieged, and Rezin executed. In accordance with his policy, Tiglath-pileser deported citizens from the conquered countries to remote areas.

Ahaz worships idols

Ahaz gained little from all this and became a mere vassal of the Assyrians. He thoroughly deserved this humiliation, for he practised the most despicable forms of idolatry, even to the extent of sacrificing his own son to the god Moloch. When he arrived at Damascus to pay homage to his lord and master he was so impressed by the heathen altar in the local shrine that he ordered Urijah, the high-priest in Jerusalem, to build a similar one in the Temple. On his return, the wicked king himself consecrated the new altar.

Pekah of Israel had also become a humble vassal of the Assyrian king. Before long, the banner of revolt was raised against him, and he was eventually assassinated by Hoshea, the son of Elah.

The prophet Hosea denounces the kingdom of Israel

The prophet Hosea, a younger contemporary of Amos, was a native of Israel. He was a living witness of the terrible events which occurred between the last years of Jeroboam II and the reign of Hoshea. Against this background, and using his own unhappy marriage as illustration — his wife having left him for her lover — Hosea accuses Israel of forsaking God for Baal. He, too, has much to say about the corrupt society of his time. 'There is no truth, nor mercy, nor knowledge of God in the land. Swearing, and lying, and killing, and stealing, and committing adultery.' By such conduct, the people had acted treacherously towards God, and were faced with the disaster of captivity.

Yet, in spite of his fierce denunciations, Hosea shows compassion and feeling for his fellow men. If only they realized the true nature of God they would have acted differently — 'My people are destroyed for lack of knowledge'. Eventually, Hosea relented and took his erring wife back. The day would come, said the prophet, when God would forgive Israel. In a famous passage he makes a passionate plea for sincere repentance, — 'Return, O Israel, unto the Lord thy God, for thou hast

140

stumbled in thine iniquity. Take with you words, and return unto the Lord'.

The Reign of Hoshea

Samaria falls to the Assyrians

Hoshea, the nineteenth and last king of Israel, was tolerated by Tiglath-pileser as long as he paid an annual tribute to his Assyrian overlord. In 728 B.C.E., Tiglath-pileser died and was succeeded by Shalmaneser IV. Hoshea thought this a good opportunity to shake off the Assyrian yoke, and turned to So, king of Egypt, for support. Egypt at that time was divided into a number of rival states, and So, one of many kings, was of no real help. Shalmaneser had Hoshea arrested and thrown into prison. He then invaded the kingdom of Israel and besieged the city of Samaria which managed to hold out for three years before it was captured. During the siege, Shalmaneser died and was succeeded by Sargon II, to whom the city fell in the year 722 B.C.E.

Sargon, in one of his inscriptions, boasts how he deported 27,290 of its inhabitants to upper Mesopotamia and Media, and appointed one of his officers governor of the city. Sargon replaced the captives taken from Samaria by foreigners from Babylon and other countries, who mingled with the remnants of the Israelite population, and continued to practise their native religions. We shall come across the descendants of the Samaritans, as they were called, soon after the return from exile (see page 173).

History would recall the great victories of Omri and Jeroboam II, but would also condemn the political intrigues and revolutions which led to Israel's downfall. Rulers and people had put their trust in Baal, the warnings of God's prophets had been ignored — the kingdom of Israel was but a memory.

***

Readings from the Bible

II Kings, chapter 16, verses 5 to 20   The Syrian-Israelite coalition
II Kings, chapter 17, verses 1 to 23   Fall of Samaria
Hosea, chapter 4, verses 1 to 3   Israel's wrongdoings
Hosea, chapter 14, verses 2 to 10   A call for repentance

Exercises

1. In whose reigns did Hosea live? Give a brief account of his prophecies.
2. Describe the events leading to the fall of the northern kingdom.
3. Name the more prominent kings of the kingdom of Israel. What were their achievements and failures?
4. Make a list of the great prophets who lived during this period. In each case give a brief summary of their teachings.

21

THE REIGN OF HEZEKIAH

Isaiah and Hezekiah

WITH the fall of Samaria, Sargon II made no attempt to overrun the kingdom of Judah, but was content, for the time being, to exact a heavy tribute from this vassal state. Historians tell us that he was busily engaged from 721 B.C.E., onward in suppressing rebellions against Assyria in Babylonia, Asia Minor and elsewhere — he could hardly spare the time or troops for campaigns of secondary importance.

In the kingdom of Judah, two outstanding figures were to dominate the scene for the next thirty years. One was the great prophet Isaiah, and the other, king Hezekiah. Isaiah, the son of Amoz, and a native of Jerusalem, received the call to be God's messenger in the year of king Uzziah's death, *c.* 740 B.C.E., and his ministry continued for over forty years, during the reigns of Jotham, Ahaz and Hezekiah. Little is known of his family background but he must have been a man of high standing as he was frequently consulted by the king and his court.

In this chapter, we shall describe Hezekiah's reforms, his attempts to free Judah from the Assyrian yoke, and the prominent part played by Isaiah in current affairs. We shall then give a summary of Isaiah's life and teachings, and refer briefly to his younger contemporary, Micah. An account of this period is to be found in the second Book of Kings, and in the Book of Isaiah. There is also the unique collection of Assyrian inscriptions discovered on the site of ancient Nineveh, which throws light on the wider historical background. The chronological

142

order of events which follows is based on all these records.

Hezekiah's
religious reforms
Hezekiah, the twelfth king of Judah, who succeeded his father Ahaz, *c.* 720 B.C.E., was a man of great piety and integrity. 'He trusted in the Lord, the God of Israel; so that after him was none like him among all the kings of Judah, nor among them that went before him.' From the very outset, Hezekiah was determined to abolish paganism and restore Judah's independence. He realized that it must take time before he achieved the latter aim but there was no obstacle in carrying out an immediate reformation. So he ordered the destruction of all heathen shrines and images, and destroyed the brass serpent, a relic of the wilderness (see page 38), which had been superstitiously revered as a god. In the month of Nisan, in the very first year of his reign, the Temple, having been thoroughly cleansed and purified, was reopened for Divine worship. In the king's presence, a solemn service of reconsecration was carried out by the reinstated priests and Levites, accompanied by sacrifices, music and song.

The celebration of
Passover
The king then decided to celebrate the Passover in Jerusalem, on the fourteenth day of the second month (i.e., Iyyar). He found it necessary to postpone the observance of this festival for a full month to give the priests enough time to prepare themselves, and to enable the people throughout the land to assemble at the Temple. Hezekiah even sent invitations to the northern tribes to participate, but the messengers were generally treated with contempt. Nevertheless, some members of the tribes of Asher, Manasseh and Zebulun joined the vast congregation of Judaeans in the Temple. The Passover was observed for seven days, and was followed by another seven days of great festivities. With renewed zeal, the people returned to their homes, and continued the destruction of shrines and images. Hezekiah then organized the Temple services, and the people resumed their offerings of tithes for the maintenance of the priests and Levites.

Egypt stirs up
trouble against
Assyria
In the years which followed Hezekiah's religious reforms, Egypt re-emerged as a united and strong power, and incited the Philistine cities to revolt against Assyria. According to one

143

of Sargon's inscriptions, Judah, Edom and Moab were invited to join a coalition. Isaiah, strongly opposed to such a move, walked about in the streets of Jerusalem, barefoot and clad in a loincloth, to indicate that support for Egypt could only result in captivity. It seems that Isaiah's counsel prevailed, for in 711 B.C.E., the revolt was crushed without Judah being involved. But the danger was only postponed. When Sennacherib succeeded his father, Sargon, in 705 B.C.E., new efforts were made by the rebel states to regain their independence.

Hezekiah recovers
from a serious
illness

About this time, Hezekiah became seriously ill, and Isaiah went to warn him, in God's name, of his approaching end. The king was greatly distressed, for there was a great deal he wanted to achieve before his death. He had not yet removed the Assyrian threat nor had he completed his task of establishing a pure system of worship centred round the Temple. Hezekiah turned his face to the wall, and wept and prayed that God should remember his efforts to serve Him. The prophet, who had only just left him, was sent back to promise that the king would recover from his illness within three days, and live a further fifteen years. Isaiah ordered a poultice of figs to be placed upon the abscess which had broken out on the king's body, and his condition improved.

The sun-dial of king
Ahaz

The assurance of a complete recovery was confirmed by a miraculous sign. In the palace courtyard stood a sun-dial, which had belonged to king Ahaz, and measured the time of day. It probably consisted of an obelisk or pole standing on the top of several steps, each representing a 'degree', on which the movement of the sun cast a shadow. As the day proceeded, the shadow would naturally lengthen. Hezekiah asked that the shadow should recede ten steps or degrees, contrary to its natural course. This request was granted, and the king composed a song of thanksgiving to God, to celebrate his recovery.

Merodach-baladan
pays Hezekiah a
visit

The news of Hezekiah's cure reached Merodach-baladan, king of Babylon, who had previously rebelled unsuccessfully against Assyria and was now seeking new allies. He sent ambassadors with gifts to call on Hezekiah, who was only too eager to show them his treasures and collection of arms, and

144

impress them with his ability to assist the Babylonians against Assyria. Isaiah censured Hezekiah for his conduct and foretold that his kingdom would fall a prey, not to Assyria, but to Babylon, the very power whose alliance he desired. This was indeed a remarkable prophecy for, though Merodach-baladan was defeated shortly afterwards by Assyria and driven from his palace, it was the Babylonians who finally stormed Jerusalem, over a hundred years later in the year 586 B.C.E.

Hezekiah rebels against Assyria

Hezekiah still sought allies to help him attack Assyria. Yielding to pressure from some of his own officers and nobles, and in spite of Isaiah's warnings, he approached Egypt to negotiate a treaty. In the year 701 B.C.E., a general revolt against Assyria broke out in the cities of Phoenicia and Philistia. Hezekiah refused to pay his annual tribute, and took immediate steps to fortify Jerusalem in preparation for the expected attack. To ensure an adequate water supply for the inhabitants, he ordered his workmen to cut a tunnel under the city and divert the water from the spring Gihon, which was outside, into a reservoir within the city walls.

The pool of Siloam

Known as the 'pool or canal of Siloam', this tunnel was accidently discovered by a party of explorers in the year 1880. They came across an inscription, written in Phoenician characters, which tells how workmen began to dig the tunnel from opposite ends and heard each other's voices when they were about five feet apart — 'and the water flowed from the spring (of Gihon) to the pool (of Siloam) for a distance of twelve hundred cubits (about eighteen hundred feet), and one hundred cubits (about one hundred and fifty feet), was the height of the rock over the heads of the excavators'.

Sennacherib invades the kingdom of Judah

Sennacherib made a lightning attack, soon crushed Judah's allies, and then made a drive towards Judah itself. Several fortified cities were captured and the Assyrians were encamped at the city of Lachish, when Hezekiah surrendered. In a message of complete submission he said, 'I have offended, withdraw from me, that which thou puttest on me will I bear'. The Assyrian imposed a penalty of three hundred talents of silver and thirty talents of gold, which Hezekiah paid by sending

Sennacherib all the sacred and royal vessels, as well as the gold on the Temple doors and pillars.

Sennacherib was so proud of his conquest of Lachish that he commissioned an artist to carve a picture of its surrender on stone. In another inscription, he tells how he conquered forty-six fortified cities of Judah, deported 200,150 people, and shut up Hezekiah in Jerusalem, 'like a bird in a cage'. He also gives details of the tribute which he imposed — precious stones, couches inlaid with ivory, elephant hides, etc.

The Rab-shakeh demands the surrender of Jerusalem

But Sennacherib's withdrawal was only temporary. He was intent on capturing Jerusalem, thereby removing the obstacle in the way of his drive towards Egypt. Some years later he resumed the attack, and his troops were once again stationed at Lachish. He then sent one of his battalions to Jerusalem under the command of the 'Tartan' (commander-in-chief), the 'Rab-saris' (chief of the princes), and the 'Rab-shakeh' (chief of the captains), apparently expecting the city's surrender without a siege. The military leaders stood outside the walls of Jerusalem and requested a parley, so Hezekiah sent three of his chief ministers to talk to them.

The Rab-shakeh and his companions

The Rab-shakeh, speaking in Hebrew, asked on whom did the king of Judah rely? Was it on Egypt, 'a bruised reed', which would pierce the hand of him who leaned on it? Was it on God? But the Lord had sent his master Sennacherib to

146

destroy Judah (probably referring to Isaiah's prophecies). Hezekiah's ministers asked him to speak in the Aramean language, so as not to be understood by the people who had assembled on the wall. They, answered the Rab-shakeh, were the very persons to whom he had been sent, to warn them of the consequences of resistance. Then, raising his voice, he cried to the men upon the wall to make their peace with him, promising they would be unharmed until the Assyrians came again to remove them to a land as good as their own. The people, on the king's previous instructions, made no reply. When Hezekiah was informed of the result of the parley, he tore his clothes as a sign of mourning, entered the Temple, and sent his ministers to Isaiah to obtain his support through prayer. The prophet told them to have no fear and declared that Sennacherib would return to his own land and there perish by the sword.

The Assyrian army is defeated

The Assyrian delegation returned to Sennacherib who was now besieging Libnah, a city in the vicinity of Lachish. Suddenly, the news came that Tirhakah of Egypt was marching against him. He was therefore forced to change his plans, and gave vent to his rage by sending Hezekiah a letter demanding complete surrender. Hezekiah spread the letter out before God in the Temple and prayed that He should prove Himself the one and only true God. The answer came through Isaiah, who prophesied that the Assyrian king would never succeed in capturing Jerusalem. That very night, through Divine intervention, the Assyrian forces suffered a terrible blow. 185,000 soldiers died as the result of a sudden plague, and the plain was covered with their corpses. Sennacherib himself returned to Assyria, and, some years later, was assassinated by two of his sons while he was worshipping in the temple of the god Nisroch. His successor was another son, Esarhaddon, one of the most powerful Assyrian kings.

Hezekiah spent the rest of his reign in peace and prosperity and, on his death, was succeeded by his son Manasseh.

The prophet Isaiah

Isaiah received his call in the year of king Uzziah's death, *c.* 740 B.C.E. In the Temple in Jerusalem he had a remarkable vision of God, seated on an immense throne, whilst the seraphim (the 'fiery' angels) proclaimed 'Holy, holy, holy is the Lord of hosts, the whole earth is full of His glory'. Then he heard God's voice saying, 'Whom shall I send, and who will go for us?' Without hesitation, Isaiah readily responded, 'Here am I, send me'. The mission with which he was entrusted required great courage, for he was to tell the people of the judgment which would overtake them because of their sins. They would be blind and deaf to all his warnings, and only after national disaster and exile had overwhelmed them would a righteous remnant be restored. Unhappily, this revelation of coming events was to be fulfilled in every detail.

Uzziah was succeeded by the god-fearing Jotham, who, after a few years, was followed by his son Ahaz, an idolater and evil-doer. Isaiah's earlier prophecies present a vivid picture of the low state into which Judah had fallen. 'Everyone worships the work of his own hands, that which his own fingers have made.' He denounced the wicked princes and judges who deprived the helpless of their rights — 'Everyone loves bribes and follows after rewards, they judge not the fatherless neither does the cause of the widow come unto them'. The rich lived in luxury, and oppressed their poorer brethren. How hypocritical it was to offer sacrifices with bloodstained hands!

During the crisis brought about by the combined attack of Rezin of Syria and Pekah of Israel (see page 139), Isaiah strongly advised Ahaz not to seek aid from Assyria, but to place his confidence in God alone. There was no need for concern since 'the riches of Damascus and the spoil of Samaria shall be carried away by the king of Assyria'. Ahaz completely ignored the prophet and, as we have seen, became a vassal of Assyria. Isaiah's prophecies were speedily fulfilled, for Damascus fell two years later, and Samaria was conquered some ten years afterwards.

The significant part played by Isaiah during Hezekiah's reign — his opposition to any revolt against Assyria, his message to the king during his illness, his censure of Hezekiah for his dealings with Merodach-baladan of Babylon and his prophecy of Sennacherib's downfall, has already been described.

'The ideal world'　　Many of Isaiah's teachings were by no means as stern as those already mentioned. During the inevitable exile, which he

148

so often spoke about, the captives would receive messages of hope and comfort, preparing them for their return to their native Homeland. His unique portrayal of the ideal world, when Peace would reign supreme, is unparalleled in prophetic literature. 'And He shall judge between the nations, and shall decide for many peoples; and they shall beat their swords into plough-shares, and their spears into pruning-hooks; nations shall not lift up sword against nation, neither shall they learn war any more.'

The prophet Micah

Micah was born in the village of Moresheth, near the Philistine border, and was a younger contemporary of Isaiah. He was equally outspoken in condemning the wealthy nobles of Jerusalem who oppressed the poor, and the hypocritical priests who were only concerned with their material gains. The man who believed in the Lord was required 'only to do justly, and to love mercy, and to walk humbly with thy God'. Like Isaiah, Micah looked forward to the distant future when mankind would live in peace and harmony, worshipping the one and only God.

Micah moved about the country warning the people of the inevitable destruction of Jerusalem and the Temple. The pious Hezekiah made no attempt to quieten the prophet's voice but, on the contrary, prayed even more earnestly that God should forgive His people's sins. This remarkable fact was referred to, over a century later, in defence of Jeremiah, who was put on trial for uttering a similar warning (see page 158).

Readings from the Bible

Isaiah, chapter 6, verses 1 to 8 — Call of Isaiah
Isaiah, chapter 2, verses 2 to 4 — The ideal World
Isaiah, chapter 11, verses 1 to 9 — The Messianic age
II Kings, chapter 19, verses 15 to 19 — Hezekiah's prayer
Isaiah, chapter 40 — A message of comfort

Exercises

1. In whose reigns did Isaiah prophesy? Why is he known as a 'major prophet? Mention four of his important teachings, and illustrate them by Biblical quotations.
2. Give an account of four historical incidents in which Isaiah played a prominent part.
3. Describe the life and times of king Hezekiah, showing clearly (*a*) his attitude towards idol worship, (*b*) his relationship to the prophet Isaiah, (*c*) his attitude towards the surrounding nations.
4. Write briefly on the following:
(*a*) the sun-dial of Ahaz; (*b*) the Siloam inscription; (*c*) the 'Rab-shakeh'.

22

THE KINGDOM OF JUDAH
(in the seventh century B.C.E.)

Kings of Judah	Approximate date of accession, B.C.E.
Manasseh	693
Amon	640
Josiah	639

The decline and fall of the Assyrian empire

A BRIEF sketch of contemporary Assyrian history will help us to understand the events which took place during the reigns of Hezekiah's successors, Manasseh, Amon, and Josiah, who occupied Judah's throne during the seventh century B.C.E. Although Sennacherib had withdrawn his armies from Judah towards the end of Hezekiah's reign, the danger of invasion had not diminished. Under Esarhaddon, Sennacherib's successor, the mighty Assyrian empire was at the height of its power. Having suppressed all Babylonian opposition, its armies advanced into Egypt, which was eventually conquered and occupied. The kingdoms en route were easily overrun and turned into vassal states. Among them, according to one of Esarhaddon's inscriptions, was Judah, under its king Manasseh, as well as Edom, Moab, and Ammon.

Assyria, however, had overreached herself. Her territorial ambitions had been realized, but she had to reckon with active resistance in practically every conquered territory. The first blows were struck during the reign of Asshurbanapal, who succeeded his father Esarhaddon *c.* 669 B.C.E. There was unrest on all sides. Babylon rebelled, and though suppressed, continued its struggle against the conqueror. Hordes of wild barbarians, including the Scythians, began to mass on Assyria's northern frontiers, whilst the Medes were threatening from the east. Assyria's military capacity was stretched to the full, and its hold on more distant countries began to weaken. Egypt felt strong enough to assert its independence about the year 655 B.C.E.

The end came after Asshurbanapal's death *c*. 633 B.C.E. His successors were unable to halt the avalanche which now swept over the tottering Assyrian empire. In 614 B.C.E., the Babylonian king Nabopolassar, assisted by the king of Media, took the offensive, and two years later besieged Nineveh and razed it to the ground. They easily overcame the feeble resistance of their common enemy who made a last stand at the city of Haran in Syria. By 609 B.C.E., Assyria's overthrow was complete.

The Reign of Manasseh

The wicked Manasseh introduces new forms of heathen worship

Manasseh, the thirteenth king of Judah, was only twelve years old when he succeeded his father Hezekiah, and his reign lasted for fifty-five years. It is clear from Esarhaddon's inscription, referred to above, that the kingdom of Judah was once again a vassal state of the Assyrian empire. Like his grandfather Ahaz, Manasseh was influenced by the idolatrous forms of worship practised by the Assyrians. Supported by the ruling classes, he readily associated himself with all that was base and evil. He restored the heathen groves which Hezekiah had removed, and re-established the worship of Baal. An idol was erected in the Temple, and altars specially built for the worship of the sun, moon and planets. The king even made his own son pass through the fire as a sacrifice to Moloch, to whom he appears to have dedicated a temple in the valley of Ben-hinnom, near Jerusalem. All forms of witchcraft were encouraged. In short, Manasseh made Judah sin to such an extent 'that they did evil more than did the nations whom the Lord destroyed before the children of Israel'.

Manasseh is carried captive to Babylon, and repents

Both king and people were warned by the prophets that, as a result, Jerusalem would be destroyed and delivered into the power of the enemy. The prophets, who denounced his crimes, and those who opposed the regime were brutally murdered. There is a tradition that Isaiah was sawn to death during the persecution. These crimes were not left unavenged. Esarhaddon found some pretext to have the king of Judah arrested and taken in chains to Babylon, where he was thrown into prison. Manasseh had sufficient time for reflection and spent his time in sincere prayer to God, pleading for forgiveness. He was eventually released from custody and, being restored to his throne, reversed his former policy. He removed the idols and altars from the Temple, repaired the sacred altar, and commanded the people to serve God.

About the year 669 B.C.E., Asshurbanapal succeeded his father as king of Assyria, but was too busily engaged with his own wars to trouble about Judah. This gave Manasseh the opportunity to strengthen Jerusalem's fortifications and station his captains at strategic points throughout the land. After his death, his son Amon ascended the throne.

Amon practises idolatry, and is assassinated

Amon, the fourteenth king of Judah, reigned for only two years, during which he reverted to the idolatrous practices of his father's earlier years. His life was cut short when he was assassinated as a result of a court conspiracy. The ringleaders were sentenced to death and Josiah, the infant son of Amon, was proclaimed king.

Reign of Josiah

Josiah abolishes idolatry

Josiah, the fifteenth king of Judah, was eight years old at his succession, and reigned for thirty-one years. During his minority, affairs of state were managed by a council of princes, and no attempt was made to abolish idolatry. But as soon as Josiah turned sixteen, he showed signs of a determination to purify religious worship. In this, he was undoubtedly influenced by such prophets as Zephaniah, who constantly warned evil-doers that 'the day of the Lord' was approaching, when all would be swept away. The gradual eclipse of Assyrian power gave Josiah a free hand and, in the twelfth year of his reign, he began to purge Jerusalem and Judah of their impurities. He himself saw to the destruction of all pagan shrines and images,

152

not only in Judah, but also throughout the territory of the former northern kingdom which he visited.

The prophet Jeremiah denounces the people's wickedness

About the year 626 B.C.E., in Josiah's thirteenth year, Jeremiah, the son of Hilkiah, began his prophetic career. He came of a priestly family living in the village of Anathoth, in the land of Benjamin. He was a young man when he received his call and fearlessly rebuked the people for their sins. 'Among my people are found wicked men . . . their houses are full of deceit . . . they plead not the cause of the fatherless.' Jeremiah attacked the false prophets and priests, who turned against God's law and misled the people. He was particularly severe in his denunciation of idolatry. Because of their treacherous conduct against God, the people of Judah were doomed, although repentance would ultimately restore them to the divine favour. We shall deal at greater length with the prophet's life and teachings in the next chapter.

The Book of the Law is discovered

Josiah must have been greatly encouraged by Jeremiah's forthright utterances, and took firm steps to carry out even greater and more important religious reforms. In the eighteenth year of his reign (*c.* 621 B.C.E.), he commissioned his chief officers to undertake a thorough repair of the Temple. The cost was met from contributions made by the people in Judah as well as by the northern tribes which the king had previously visited. During the reigns of Manasseh and Amon, when the Temple was neglected, the holy scrolls had probably been destroyed. In the course of the repairs, Hilkiah, the High Priest, discovered a written scroll which, on examination, proved to be a copy of the Book of the Law. The High Priest handed it to Shaphan the royal scribe, who took it to Josiah and read it to him.

There are several passages in the Torah, such as Leviticus, chapter 26 and Deuteronomy, chapter 28, which set out the dreadful punishments for disobedience to God's commandments. When Josiah heard them, he tore his clothes in sorrow, for he realized that the sinful conduct of his predecessors and of the people would bring about inevitable disaster. Josiah told Hilkiah, Shaphan and others to consult Huldah, the prophetess, who lived in Jerusalem, as to whether the Divine judgments would be fulfilled. Her reply confirmed his worst fears. The evils foretold in the Book of the Law would come upon the nation, but as the king has shown such genuine grief, they would not occur during his lifetime.

Josiah carries out sweeping religious reforms

Josiah immediately set about to avert, if possible, God's anger and convened a general assembly of all his subjects in the Temple courtyard. Having read to them every word of the scroll, he and the people pledged themselves before God to keep His commandments, testimonies and statutes. With renewed zeal a more thorough religious reformation was undertaken. The king destroyed all the idols in the Temple, and the heathen altars built by Ahaz and Manasseh were beaten into the dust, which was scattered over the brook of Kidron. The valley of Ben-hinnom, the centre of child sacrifice to the god Moloch, was ploughed over and used as a rubbish heap. Josiah banned all forms of superstitious practices. He next went to Bethel and pulled down the altar erected by Jeroboam, together with the idol of Astarte.

The Passover is celebrated

Josiah celebrated the festival of Passover during the month of Nisan, in accordance with the directions in this newly discovered Book of the Law. The ark was replaced in the Holy of Holies, from which it had perhaps been removed during the repairs. The priests and Levites were told to carry out their duties in accordance with the Law, and the king and his princes presented gifts of cattle to all those who had assembled at the Temple, for the peace-offerings to be made during the week. The paschal sacrifice was offered and the festival was celebrated for seven days, 'and there was no Passover like to that kept in Israel from the days of Samuel the prophet'. This was the last great act of united worship before the captivity.

Josiah meets his death at Megiddo

Whilst Josiah was engaged in carrying out his religious reforms, Assyria was fighting for its life against Babylonia. In the year 609 B.C.E., as mentioned above (see page 151), the Assyrians were making a final stand at Haran. Pharaoh-necho of Egypt feared the might of Babylonia, which, after its military successes, would undoubtedly sweep towards the Nile. He therefore marched to Carchemish on the Euphrates to

154

assist the Assyrians in their desperate plight. Josiah had no desire to assist Assyria in regaining its power, and was determined to check Egypt's advance. Pharaoh-necho sent him an emphatic but friendly warning not to interfere. Josiah ignored this warning and engaged the Egyptian army in battle, in the plains of Megiddo. Disguised as an ordinary soldier, the king joined his troops but was mortally wounded by a shot from an Egyptian archer. His servants brought him to Jerusalem where he died and was buried, greatly mourned by his people. Jeremiah the prophet was deeply distressed at the pious king's death and composed a special funeral elegy in honour of the man who had tried so hard to bring his people back to God.

Readings from the Bible

II Chronicles, chapter 33 — Reign of Manasseh
II Kings, chapter 22, verses 8 to 20 — Discovery of the Book of the Law
II Kings, chapter 23, verses 21 to 25 — Josiah's Passover
II Chronicles, chapter 35, verses 20 to 27 — Josiah's death

Exercises

1. Give a brief account of the Assyrian menace to the kingdoms of Israel and Judah.
2. What were the reforms introduced by king Josiah?
3. Mention the occasions in the Bible when special mention is made of the Passover being observed. Write more fully on two of them.

23

DECLINE AND FALL OF THE SOUTHERN KINGDOM

Kings of Judah	Approximate dates of accession, B.C.E.
Jehoahaz	609
Jehoiakim	608
Jehoiachin	598
Zedekiah	597

The life and teachings of Jeremiah

AFTER Josiah's death, Judah's position rapidly deteriorated. The dramatic events which unfolded themselves up to the final fall of Jerusalem are, for the most part, described in the Book of Jeremiah, which supplements the information to be found in the second Book of Kings and in the second Book of Chronicles. In addition, a number of Babylonian texts have been published in recent years, adding to our knowledge of the period.

Jeremiah's earlier prophecies have already been mentioned (see pages 153 and 155). During the reigns of Josiah's successors, the prophet's voice was heard incessantly, foretelling the conquest of a once proud nation by the Babylonians. His constant companion and disciple, Baruch, fortunately recorded his master's prophecies and so made them available for all time. We shall now deal briefly with Jeremiah's life and teachings, set against the background of contemporary history, and in conjunction with the reigns of the last kings of Judah.

The Reign of Jehoahaz

Pharaoh-necho deposes Jehoahaz and deports him to Egypt

Pharaoh-necho, after defeating Josiah's forces (see page 155), marched on to Haran, but the Babylonian's army proved too powerful. The king of Egypt retired to Riblah, in central Syria,

156

determined at all costs to become absolute lord of all the territory between Syria and Egypt, including, of course, the kingdom of Judah.

Meanwhile, Jehoahaz, Josiah's youngest son (also known as Shallum), was proclaimed king by popular choice. During the brief three months of his reign as sixteenth king of Judah, he re-introduced all the old evils of idolatry. Pharaoh-necho, refusing to recognize Jehoahaz, summoned him to Riblah, kept him a prisoner, and carried him off to Egypt, where he died soon afterwards. In his place, the Pharaoh put Jehoahaz's stepbrother Eliakim on the throne, and, to show his authority, changed the new king's name to Jehoiakim. He also imposed a fine of a hundred talents of silver and a talent of gold on the country.

Jeremiah had little sympathy for the weak and wicked Jehoahaz: 'Weep sore for him that goeth away,' he proclaimed, 'for he shall return no more, nor see his native country'.

The Reign of Jehoiakim

Jeremiah's life is endangered

Jehoiakim, the seventeenth king of Judah, was twenty-five years old when he was placed on the throne by Pharaoh-necho, and reigned for eleven years. This Egyptian vassal showed every contempt for the true prophets and was steeped in idolatry. From the very commencement of Jehoiakim's reign, Jeremiah sternly rebuked his injustice and greed, mentioning especially his reckless extravagance in building himself a magnificent palace, and contrasting all this with king Josiah's regard for the poor. Jeremiah was equally forthright in denouncing the sinful priests, prophets and, indeed, the whole nation for worshipping idols. On one occasion he stood in the Temple court reproaching the people for their evil, when Pashhur, the chief officer of the Temple, struck him and had him put in the stocks. On his release the next day, Jeremiah foretold the captivity of Judah by Babylon. Pashhur, he said, would be among the prisoners and would die in exile.

On another occasion, the prophet declared that God would not bring the threatened evil if the people repented; otherwise, the Temple would be destroyed like the tabernacle at Shiloh (see page 64). The priests and prophets were resolved that

Jeremiah should die, and prosecuted him before a tribunal of princes for blasphemy. Jeremiah strenuously denied the accusation and claimed that he spoke in God's name. Fortunately, he was defended by certain elders who recalled the days of king Hezekiah, when the prophet Micah prophesied the fall of Jerusalem, but was not punished (see page 149). Jeremiah's life was finally saved by the advocacy of Ahikam, the son of Josiah's scribe, Shaphan.

Jehoiakim is forced to pay tribute to Babylon

Meanwhile the struggle for supremacy between Egypt and Babylon continued. In 605 B.C.E., Nebuchadnezzar of Babylon, the son and general of Nabopolassar, inflicted a heavy defeat on the Egyptian forces at Carchemish, forcing them to flee to their own country. This blow put an end to the hopes of the Egyptian party in Jerusalem, and left the city defenceless. The Babylonian general did not attack Jerusalem immediately, as he was recalled home to be crowned king in place of his father who had died. The following year he resumed his campaign and Jehoiakim had no option but to transfer his allegiance and pay tribute to his new master. This prompt submission saved Judah from invasion.

Jehoiakim destroys the scroll containing Jeremiah's prophecies

After his trial, Jeremiah had been forbidden access to the Temple. So he dictated to Baruch, the son of Neriah, all the prophecies he had delivered since the days of Josiah, against Israel, Judah, and other nations, hoping that, on hearing them, the people would repent. He told Baruch to read the scroll to an assembly gathered in the Temple courtyard to observe a special fast day. Baruch did so, and Micaiah, Shaphan's grandson, was so impressed that he interrupted a council meeting of the princes and gave them a report of what had happened. The princes sent for Baruch and asked him to read the scroll again. They then advised him and Jeremiah to go into hiding while they informed the king. Jehoiakim was sitting in his winter palace, and, at his command, prince Jehudi read from the scroll. As fast as he read, the king cut the leaves with a penknife and defiantly threw them into the fire burning in a brazier, till the whole volume was consumed. Jehoiakim gave orders for Jeremiah and Baruch to be arrested, but they were nowhere to be found. When Jeremiah heard about the burning of the scroll, he re-dictated his prophecies to Baruch, adding a special condemnation of Jehoiakim's sins.

Jehoiakim rebels against Nebuchadnezzar

In 601 B.C.E., Jehoiakim recklessly rebelled against Nebuchadnezzar. The Babylonian king was occupied elsewhere, but, for two years, he sent advance forces of such troops as he could spare, together with those from his vassal kingdoms of Syria, Moab and Ammon, all of whom kept the southern kingdom in a state of turmoil. Finally, in 598 B.C.E., Nebuchadnezzar arrived with his main force and besieged Jerusalem. Jehoiakim's reliance on Egyptian aid, which was not forthcoming, had proved fatal, and as the enemy surrounded the city's walls Jehoiakim fell ill and died.

The Reign of Jehoiachin

Jehoiachin is taken captive to Babylon

Jehoiachin, Jehoiakim's son, and the eighteenth king of Judah, was eighteen years old when he came to the throne. Jeremiah's comments on this idolatrous king were significant — 'And I will cast thee out, and thy mother that bore thee, into another country, where ye were not born, and there shall ye die'. With the mighty Nebuchadnezzar at Jerusalem's gates, there was little the king could do. After a siege of three months, Jehoiachin, together with the queen-mother, the princes, the leading citizens, seven thousand warriors and one thousand craftsmen, were all taken as captives to Babylon — among them the prophet Ezekiel (see page 166). In this way Nebuchadnezzar made certain that no one capable of organizing any further resistance was left behind. He also plundered the Temple and palace of their treasures, leaving the country impoverished and helpless. The king had no quarrel with Jeremiah, who was allowed to remain behind. Finally, Mattaniah, another son of Josiah, and uncle of Jehoiachin, was made king over the remnant of Judah, under his new name of Zedekiah.

Jehoiachin survived for many years after the fall of Jerusalem. He was eventually released from prison by Evilmerodach, king of Babylon, who succeeded Nebuchadnezzar in the year 562 B.C.E., and was treated kindly for the rest of his life, being granted a daily allowance for his maintenance, and the privilege of having his meals at the royal table.

Zedekiah warns the king against an alliance with Egypt

Zedekiah, the nineteenth and last king of Judah, was twenty years old at his accession, and reigned eleven years, until the final destruction of Jerusalem. This weak-willed king could not make up his mind whether to take Jeremiah's advice and submit to Babylonian authority, or to side with his nobles and form an alliance with Egypt, which was waiting to wipe out the disgrace of the defeat at Carchemish. Egypt had undoubtedly sent secret agents to Judah and elsewhere, to incite the vassal kingdoms to revolt. One prophet, Hananiah, went so far as to declare that Jehoiachin and the Babylonian exiles would return within two years. Jeremiah could only repeat his warning that such wild talk could only make matters worse. In a famous letter addressed to the exiles, Jeremiah told them not to listen to the false prophets in their midst with their promises of a speedy return, but to settle down peacefully, and try and live a normal life. In God's name he announced that deliverance would come after an exile lasting seventy years.

Zedekiah rebels against Babylon

In the fourth year of his reign (c. 593 B.C.E.), Zedekiah paid a visit of homage to Nebuchadnezzar, perhaps to allay any suspicions of disloyalty which may have been aroused. The secret understanding with Egypt continued, however, and when Pharaoh-hophra came to the throne in the year 588 B.C.E., Zedekiah openly rebelled against the king of Babylon. The prophet Ezekiel (see page 166), tells us that Zedekiah sent his ambassadors to Egypt to ask for horses and soldiers, thereby breaking his oath of allegiance to Nebuchadnezzar. The Babylonian army immediately marched through the kingdom of Judah, and once again Jerusalem was besieged. Zedekiah, in despair, turned to Jeremiah, only to be told that he and the people would be delivered into the enemy's hands.

Jeremiah is arrested and imprisoned

Surprisingly, Pharaoh-hophra led a powerful army to Jerusalem in aid of his ally, and the Babylonians were forced to withdraw. The pro-Egyptian party was triumphant — Jeremiah had prophesied falsely! But the prophet gave the warning, 'Pharaoh's army shall return to Egypt . . . and the Chaldeans shall come again'. One day, while Jeremiah was about to leave

160

Jerusalem to visit his home town of Anathoth, he was arrested on a charge of desertion to the enemy and imprisoned in the cells. He appealed to Zedekiah for mercy and was transferred to the court of the guard, where conditions were much better. The princes intervened and demanded Jeremiah's death on the pretext that he was discouraging the army and people by his constant denunciations. Jeremiah was flung into a pit and would have died of hunger had he not been rescued, with the king's permission, by Ebed-melech, an Ethiopian officer. Zedekiah arranged to meet Jeremiah secretly and pressed him to reveal the outcome of the siege. The prophet could only advise surrender, if the king wished to live and save Jerusalem from destruction. Zedekiah begged Jeremiah to keep the interview a secret and sent him back to the court of the guard, where he remained until Jerusalem was taken.

Within a few months, the Babylonians renewed their attack with a massive force, and Pharaoh-hophra was forced to return to Egypt.

Jerusalem falls

Apart from this short pause, Jerusalem had been besieged for eighteen months, and severe famine was causing untold misery. The defenders were too weak to hold out much longer. In the fourth month (Tammuz), of the year 586 B.C.E., the city walls were breached. During the night, Zedekiah and his officers escaped through the garden gate of the royal palace but were overtaken and captured in the plains of Jericho, some fifteen miles away. Zedekiah was brought to Nebuchadnezzar at Riblah and forced to witness the slaughter of his own sons and princes. His eyes were put out and he was sent to Babylon, where he remained a close prisoner till the day of his death.

Meanwhile, the king of Babylon decided to destroy the rebellious city, which he had twice spared. A month later, on the seventh day of the fifth month (Ab), Nebuzaradan, the Babylonian commander-in-chief, arrived at Jerusalem to carry out the instructions of his royal master. The Temple, the royal palace, and the principal houses were set on fire, and the city walls levelled to the ground. All the sacred vessels in the Temple were removed and the two great pillars of the Temple porch, Jachin and Boaz, and the brass 'sea' (see page 95), were broken into pieces and carried as scrap-metal to Babylon. Four thousand six hundred citizens, in all, were rounded up for deportation, and seventy leaders, including Seraiah, the High Priest, were sent to Riblah, where they were executed.

Captives being led into exile

A poetical account of this national disaster is to be found in the Book of Lamentations, written, according to tradition, by the prophet Jeremiah.

Gedaliah is appointed governor of Judah

In accordance with his usual policy, Nebuchadnezzar appointed a native of the conquered country as governor. His choice fell on Gedaliah, whose father Ahikam had once saved Jeremiah's life (see page 158). Gedaliah took up his residence at Mizpah, near Jerusalem, where he was joined by Jeremiah. The prophet had been among the captives rounded up in Jerusalem, but was released by Nebuzaradan when the column of prisoners reached Ramah, five miles north of the city. Given the option of either going to Babylon or remaining behind, Jeremiah chose to stay at Mizpah. The dispersed soldiers and people began to gather round their new governor, who advised them to live quietly as the subjects of the Babylonian king. Then refugees returned from the countries of Moab, Ammon, and Edom, and the people were soon peacefully engaged in gathering the vintage and summer fruits throughout their cities.

Gedaliah is assassinated

Unhappily, this peaceful interlude did not last long. Baalis, the Ammonite king, was determined to hinder the development of the small Jewish colony. He therefore incited Ishmael, the son of Nethaniah, and a descendant of the house of David, to assassinate Gedaliah. Ishmael may well have felt resentful at

162

being passed over as governor. Gedaliah was warned of the danger by Johanan, one of his devoted officers, but refused to believe that such treachery was possible. Two months after Nebuzaradan's departure, Ishmael, with ten of his friends, joined Gedaliah at a meal in Mizpah. They suddenly attacked the governor and killed him, together with his Jewish and Babylonian bodyguard. A few days later, they murdered seventy pilgrims on their way to the ruined site of the Temple.

Jeremiah is taken forcibly to Egypt

Ishmael then left Mizpah for Ammon, taking with him a number of captives including Zedekiah's daughters, who had been entrusted to Gedaliah's care. He was hotly pursued by Johanan and his fellow officers, who overtook him at Gibeon, and rescued the captives. Ishmael, however, with eight of his men, managed to escape. Fearing Nebuchadnezzar's vengeance for the murder of his governor, Johanan and his party decided to take refuge in Egypt. They stayed a while near Bethlehem and asked Jeremiah for his advice. After ten days, the answer came, promising God's protection if they remained, and warning them that if they went to Egypt, sword and famine would overtake them. The prophet's warning only resulted in a charge being made against him of conspiring with Baruch to hand them over to the Babylonians. Jeremiah and Baruch were forcibly taken to Egypt, and the emigrants reached Tahpanhes, on the Egyptian frontier. Before long, Jewish communities were established in a number of cities, including Migdol and Memphis.

The prophet's last years gave him no happiness. The Jews in Egypt completely ignored the lessons of the past, and payed homage to heathen idols, especially to the goddess Ishtar, known as 'the queen of heaven'. All Jeremiah's entreaties were in vain, and his last warnings fell on deaf ears. The Bible does not record the prophet's death, but doubtless he died in Egypt. Let us leave this courageous and outspoken prophet by quoting one of his comforting messages, in which he promised national restoration — 'There is hope for thy future, saith the Lord; and thy children shall return to their own border'.

Readings from	Jeremiah, chapter 1	Jeremiah's call
the Bible	Jeremiah, chapter 26	Jeremiah is put on trial
	Jeremiah, chapter 29, verses 1 to 9	Jeremiah writes to the exiles
	II Kings, chapter 25	Capture of Jerusalem
	Jeremiah, chapters 40 and 41	The story of Gedaliah
	Book of Lamentations, chapter 1	A national disaster

Exercises

1. Mention five important incidents in Jeremiah's career. Write briefly on three of them.
2. Give an account of Jeremiah's attitude towards the kings of Judah and their foreign policies.
3. Describe the fall of Jerusalem.
4. When is the Book of Lamentations read in the Synagogue and why?
5. It has been said that Zedekiah was a weak and indecisive king. Is this true?
6. Write briefly on the following:
   (*a*) Jehoahaz of Judah; (*b*) Jehoiachin; (*c*) Gedaliah.

24

THE BABYLONIAN EXILE

The Jewish dispersion

AFTER the fall of Jerusalem in 586 B.C.E., Jewish communities were to be found in at least three different countries.

In the former kingdom of Israel

(i) Descendants of the ten tribes still occupied the territory of the former northern kingdom, which had been conquered by Sargon in 722 B.C.E. (see page 141). Their main centre was Samaria but, through intermarriage with foreign settlers whom the Assyrians had brought in from other territories, they became a mixed race. As a result, pagan forms of worship were introduced, side by side with the worship of God. The Samaritans, as they were called, had little contact with their southern neighbours in spite of Josiah's efforts to win them back (see page 152), and they reappear on the scene about the year 536 B.C.E.

In the former kingdom of Judah

In the former southern kingdom of Judah, the majority of those left behind by the Babylonians were poor and un-educated Jews incapable of organizing any revolt. Deprived of leadership, they could do little but wait in hope for the restoration promised by the prophets.

In Egypt

(ii) A number of Jewish refugees came to Egypt. After Gedaliah's assassination, they settled in Tahpanhes and other cities, came under the influence of pagan worship (see page 163), and seem to have been quite content to adapt themselves to their new conditions.

165

(iii) Without doubt, the survival of the Jewish people was due to the exiles in Babylon, numbering about 4,600. They had witnessed the fulfilment of Jeremiah's prophecies and were convinced that the prophet's promise of return to their Homeland was but a matter of time. Many of them had previously occupied important positions in the civil and religious field, and were determined to preserve their identity as Jews. The man of the hour was the prophet Ezekiel, from whose writings we are able to reconstruct their life in exile.

The life and teachings of the prophet Ezekiel

Ezekiel, the son of Buzi the priest, was the first prophet to live and prophesy in exile. As a young man he lived in Jerusalem and was well acquainted with every detail of the Temple ritual. During the reign of Jehoiachin, he was an eye-witness of the events leading up to the king's surrender in 597 B.C.E. (see page 159), and he himself was among the captives carried off to Babylon. Nebuchadnezzar was an astute ruler, and his general policy was to allow his captives some measure of self-government, thereby diminishing the danger of rebellion. The main body of exiled Jews was allotted a sizeable tract of land at a place called Tel-Abib, on the banks of the Chebar canal, which watered the town of Nippur.

In the year 593 B.C.E., five years after Jehoiachin's captivity, the prophetic inspiration suddenly came to Ezekiel while he was walking by the river Chebar. In a remarkable vision he became aware of God's glory; he saw a chariot borne on four wheels with four living creatures alongside, each combining the likeness of a man, lion, ox and eagle. He heard God's voice appointing him 'a watchman unto the House of Israel'. His immediate task was to warn the sinful kingdom of Judah of its inevitable doom. Ezekiel then went to live in Tel-Abib where, for nearly six years, he condemned the corruption in Jerusalem, which was encouraged by Zedekiah and his court. In one of his visions, the prophet saw himself standing in the Temple court, witnessing a number of degrading scenes. The Temple walls were covered with carvings of idols, and, in one of the inner rooms, seventy prominent leaders were secretly engaged in idolatrous practices. Elsewhere, the women sat 'weeping for Tammuz' — the god of vegetation, who, according to legend,

166

vanished each summer into the underworld and returned the following spring.

Ezekiel's use of symbols

Ezekiel, in order to drive his lesson home, often portrayed coming events through symbolic acts. On one occasion he drew a plan of the Jerusalem siege, and ate inferior bread, as a sign of famine. On another, he dug a hole through the wall of his house and left at night with a knapsack on his back, to symbolize Zedekiah's efforts to escape (see page 161). Strange though these demonstrations must have been to the exiles, Ezekiel's prestige increased when the final blow fell and Zedekiah was brought in chains to Babylon in the year 586 B.C.E.

From a number of passages in the Book of Ezekiel, we learn that the prophet's house was the meeting-place of the elders who represented the Jewish exiles, and who often visited the prophet for instruction in the Law. Ezekiel laid great stress on the importance of observing the commandments, and frequently refers to the holiness of the Sabbath and Festivals. The people, far from being treated as slaves, were allowed to cultivate their land. In the course of time they became prosperous, and were able to make substantial contributions towards the restoration of the Temple (see page 171).

The valley of dry bones

Ezekiel continued to prophesy some fifteen years after Jerusalem had fallen. His promise for the future was most encouraging, for he was certain that the exiles would return to their own homeland and form a united nation. One of his most familiar parables is known as 'the vision of the valley of dry bones'. The prophet found himself carried into a valley of dry bones, symbolizing the defeated Jewish people. At God's bidding he ordered the bones to be covered with flesh and come to life. So, he proclaimed, would the Jewish nation return from the grave of exile to its former splendour. In anticipation he prepared a plan for the new Jerusalem and, with careful detail, drew up a blueprint of the future Temple, going as far as to give its exact measurements. In this way he instilled new hope into the hearts of the Jewish exiles and repeatedly encouraged them with the assurance that their sins would be forgiven, if they repented.

The story of Daniel   The experiences in exile of a group of young, pious, and intelligent Jews are described in the biblical book of Daniel. Together with three of his companions, Daniel was taken from his home in Judah and brought up in the royal court. Daniel and his friends remained loyal to their faith and refused to partake of any food forbidden by Jewish law. In this book we find the familiar stories of 'Daniel in the lions' den' and of how Shadrach,

Daniel in the lions' den

Meshach and Abednego who, because they would not worship a golden image, were thrown into a furnace. In each case, the young men were delivered from danger. Daniel was able to interpret the weird dreams troubling King Nebuchadnezzar, and was promoted to a position of high rank in the royal service.

Decline and fall of Babylon   Throughout Nebuchadnezzar's long reign (605 - 562 B.C.E.), the Babylonian empire had reached the height of its power and prosperity. There seemed little chance of a change in policy, which would allow the exiles to rejoin their fellow-Jews at home. The dramatic events following the king's death raised new hopes. His son, Evil-merodach, released Jehoiachin, the exiled king of Judah, from prison (see page 159), but was assassinated after a short reign of two years by Neriglassar, one of his officers. Further changes of rulers and dynasties followed, and in the year 555 B.C.E. we find the usurper Nabonidus on the throne. This monarch committed a serious blunder by interfering with the ancient religious beliefs of his people, and thereby antagonized the priests. For eight years he preferred to live

168

at Teima in the Arabian desert, leaving his son Belshazzar in charge of home affairs. King and people were no longer united.

The 'writing on the wall'

It was during Belshazzar's reign that the famous incident of the 'writing on the wall' took place. Belshazzar made a lavish feast for his nobles, and they drank wine from the gold and silver vessels taken by Nebuchadnezzar when he plundered the holy Temple. The fingers of a man's hand suddenly appeared and wrote a mysterious message on the palace walls. Belshazzar was terrified and promised the greatest honours to any of his astrologers who could interpret its meaning. None could do so. Daniel was then called, and he alone was able to reveal the implication of the message which read, '*Mene, mene, tekel upharsin*'. These were four Aramaic words, each of which contained a hidden warning for Belshazzar. *Mene*, God has numbered your kingdom and brought it to an end. *Tekel*, you are weighed in the balances, and are found wanting. *Upharsin*, (and) your kingdom is divided, and given to the Medes and Persians. The promised reward was bestowed upon Daniel, and, that very night, according to the Biblical narrative, Belshazzar was slain.

Babylon is overthrown by Cyrus of Persia

The final blow came when Babylonia was invaded by Cyrus, king of the Medes and Persians. This Cyrus, a former vassal king of Media, had led a successful revolt against his overlord, and, supported by the army, soon achieved tremendous military power. Cyrus' forces thundered westwards, and in 539 B.C.E. his general Gobryas entered Babylon without striking a blow, and Nabonidus was taken prisoner.

These momentous events are recorded on a broken cylinder of baked clay called the 'Cyrus Cylinder', where the conqueror tells how he made a ceremonial entry into the capital. 'All the people and governors', he writes, 'kissed his feet and rejoiced in him as king.' Cyrus soon proved himself an enlightened ruler. He treated his newly-acquired subjects with generosity and leniency, and did not interfere with their religious way of life. He even allowed their leaders to participate in the administration of their native cities, under the supervision of Persian governors. The Jewish exiles in Babylon waited breathlessly for some favourable gesture — they were not disappointed.

———————⟫•⟪———————

Readings from the Bible

Ezekiel, chapter 1	Ezekiel's vision
Ezekiel, chapter 37, verses 1 to 14	'The valley of dry bones'
Psalm 137	'By the rivers of Babylon'

Exercises

1. Why did the people of the northern kingdom disappear during their exile and why did the Judaeans survive and return?
2. Mention four of Ezekiel's teachings and write about two of them.
3. Summarize the 'vision of the valley of dry bones' and explain its application.
4. Read the book of Daniel, chapters 3, 5 and 6. Tell, in your own words, the stories of the fiery furnace, Daniel in the lions' den, and 'the writing on the wall'.

25

THE RETURN

FROM the fall of Babylon in 539 B.C.E., until the year 333 B.C.E., when Alexander the Great decisively defeated the Persians at the battle of Issus in Syria, the Jewish people remained under Persian domination. The events described in the remaining chapters of this book took place during the reigns of the following kings:

B.C.E.		B.C.E.	
538-529	Cyrus	521-486	Darius I
529-522	Cambyses	486-465	Xerxes I (Ahasuerus)
522-521	Gaumata (a usurper)	464-424	Artaxerxes I

Cyrus issues his famous proclamation

In 538 B.C.E., the first year of his Babylonian conquest, Cyrus issued his famous proclamation, allowing his Jewish subjects,

Cyrus' Proclamation

wherever they lived, to return to Jerusalem and rebuild the Temple. He requested their fellow-citizens to assist the venture by contributions of gold, goods and cattle. The response to this

171

act of noble generosity by the Babylonian exiles was immediate, and the necessary preparations were soon made. Zerubbabel, of the royal house of David, assisted by ten of his chosen friends and Joshua, the High Priest, led the expedition. Cyrus instructed his treasurer, Mithredath, to hand over to Zerubbabel 5,400 sacred vessels seized by Nebuchadnezzar when he plundered the Temple. The total number who volunteered to return came to 42,360, including 4,289 priests and 341 Levites. They brought with them horses, mules, camels and asses and set out on the long and difficult journey undertaken centuries before by their ancestor, Abraham.

The Persian Empire

The foundation stones of the second Temple are laid

On arriving in Judah, they settled in a number of cities, especially in and around Jerusalem. All the Jews assembled in Jerusalem in the seventh month of the year (Tishri) so that they might again observe the daily sacrifices, as prescribed in the Law of Moses. The sacred altar was rebuilt, and the Feast of Tabernacles joyously observed on the fifteenth day of Tishri. It is interesting to recall that this was the very festival on which Solomon dedicated the first Temple (see page 96). No time was lost in setting the wheels in motion. Carpenters and masons were engaged, and Phoenician workmen were hired to transport cedar-trees from Lebanon to Jaffa, as in Solomon's day.

In the second month of the following year — Iyyar, 537 B.C.E. — the foundation stones were laid with great solemnity, to the accompaniment of music and singing. But the shouts of the people were mingled with the tears of the priests and old men who had seen the first Temple in all its splendour, so that

172

the cries of joy could hardly be distinguished from those of sadness.

The Samaritans prevent the work of rebuilding the Temple

The work of rebuilding the Temple soon came to a standstill, The Samaritans, descendants of the heathen settlers brought into the northern kingdom by the Assyrians (see page 141) expressed a desire to assist in rebuilding the Temple. Zerub, babel and his associates, who regarded them as idolaters. contemptuously refused the offer, and the Samaritans, embittered by this rebuff, succeeded in preventing further building operations. They bribed Persian agents to make false accusations of disloyalty against the Jews and discouraged the workmen with their insults. As a result, the work was held up, while these complaints were being investigated.

Cyrus seems to have been too busy with his own affairs to intervene in the dispute, and the discouraged Jews began to lose their enthusiasm. They felt the time could be better spent by building homes for themselves and earning a livelihood. During the next fifteen years (535 - 520 B.C.E.), not a single stone was added to the structure. Cyrus was succeeded by his son Cambyses (529 - 522 B.C.E.), who was deposed by the usurper, Gaumata. Shortly afterwards, Darius, son of Hystaspes, and a member of the royal family, overthrew Gaumata and executed him.

Darius gives permission for the completion of the Temple

We resume our story in 520 B.C.E., in the second year of Darius' reign. The king at that time was occupied in suppressing revolts within his empire, and the future of the Persian empire was in the balance. The prophets Haggai and Zechariah considered this an opportune moment to rekindle the enthusiasm of the Jews to restore the Temple, as the symbol of God's supremacy over all mankind, and urged Zerubbabel and Joshua to rouse the people to action. Before long the Temple site was once again the centre of great activity.

Eighteen years had passed since Cyrus' proclamation and the local authorities seemed totally unaware of its existence. Tattenai, the Persian governor in charge of Judea, therefore intervened to enquire on whose authority the Temple was being constructed. On receiving the reply that this had been authorized by Cyrus, Tattenai wrote a letter to king Darius asking him to find out the facts by searching the royal records. The search was accordingly made and the original document was discovered in the royal archives at Ecbatana, the summer residence of the Persian kings. Darius not only ratified the edict of his predecessor, but ordered his officials to contribute money, material, and even animals for sacrifice. He also threatened to impose the severest penalties on anyone who did not carry out his wishes.

Dedication of the Temple

So the work continued and prospered with the constant encouragement of the prophets Haggai and Zechariah. The Temple was completed on the third of Adar in the year 516 B.C.E. At the dedication ceremony, sacrifices were offered on behalf of the twelve tribes, a decisive proof that the returned exiles considered themselves representatives of the whole House of Israel. The priests and Levites were given their sacred duties and, in the following month of Nisan, the Passover was celebrated with great joy.

The story of Esther

Darius I was succeeded in 486 B.C.E., by Xerxes. Many scholars identify this monarch with king Ahasuerus, whose consort was Queen Esther. This view seems to be supported by the account given of this king and his times by Herodotus, the

Mordecai rides in triumph

Greek historian. In his famous chronicles, Herodotus describes Xerxes as 'vain, selfish, fickle, and hot-headed' — characteristics which tally with those of Ahasuerus. The courageous stand of the Jewish queen and her cousin Mordecai against the wicked Haman is told in the Book of Esther. Through Divine

174

Providence, the Persian Jews were delivered from the danger that threatened them.

The Samaritans again intervene, and prevent the rebuilding of the city walls

Xerxes died in 465 B.C.E., and was succeeded by Artaxerxes I. Some fifty years had passed since the completion of the Temple, and the Jews now decided to rebuild Jerusalem's walls and repair its foundations. But they still had to contend with the hostility of their enemies. Early in his reign, Artaxerxes received a letter from Rehum, head of the Samaritan community, accusing the Jews of rebellious intentions. They were rebuilding the walls, he wrote, in order to seize independence. In his reply, Artaxerxes called Jerusalem a rebellious city and issued an order for all building to cease. Rehum and his companions immediately hurried to Jerusalem and forcibly compelled the Jews to obey the king's command.

The prophet Malachi reveals a serious state of affairs

As a result, the Jews became so despondent that they began to be indifferent towards their religious responsibilities. Malachi, the last of 'the Twelve Prophets', was aghast at the situation which had developed. His prophecies reveal that even the priests showed utter contempt for their sacred duties by sacrificing blemished animals on the altar. A number of people had committed the grave sin of divorcing their Jewish wives to marry foreign women. Yet, in spite of all these evils, Malachi was confident that righteousness would triumph in the end.

Ezra, the scribe, receives permission to visit Jerusalem

Although Artaxerxes had forbidden the Jews to rebuild the fortifications of Jerusalem, he continued the traditional policy of his predecessors and did not interfere with their religious practices. In Babylon itself, the Jewish community was well-organized. Much time was spent in the study of the Torah and on its interpretation, and copies of the sacred text were carefully transcribed for use at religious assemblies. Instruction was in the hands of the *Sopherim*, i.e., Scribes, distinguished for their knowledge of the Scriptures, whose task it was to educate the masses to understand and practise God's commandments. The chief Scribe, recognized as such by the Persian government, was Ezra, the Priest, who could trace his descent from Aaron, the first High Priest.

Ezra had set his heart on teaching the law of God to his coreligionists in Israel. In the seventh year of Artaxerxes' reign (458 B.C.E.), he asked for the king's consent to go to Jerusalem with authority to take complete control of religious affairs. Artaxerxes immediately agreed and handed Ezra a letter, which included a number of generous requests. Artaxerxes not only gave permission to all Israelites, priests and Levites in his realm, who so wished, to accompany Ezra on his mission, but he and his counsellors, as a token of goodwill, presented considerable gifts of money to purchase animals for sacrifice, and vessels for use in the Temple. Furthermore, all the treasurers beyond the Euphrates were commanded to supply Ezra's needs, and to exempt the priests, Levites and those who ministered in the Temple from paying taxes. Ezra was empowered to appoint magistrates and judges, with authority to punish all who disobeyed God's law.

Ezra and his followers arrive safely

Nearly fifteen hundred Jews availed themselves of the king's permission to return and, led by Ezra, left Babylon. They encamped for three days at Ahava, one of the Babylonian canals, where Ezra was joined by a number of Levites. Ashamed to ask the king for a military escort during the dangerous journey, Ezra proclaimed a fast and prayed for Divine protection. After four months they arrived safely in Jerusalem, and Ezra handed the treasures and vessels to Meremoth, son of Uriah the priest. Sacrifices were offered by the returned exiles, and the king's instructions were delivered to the Persian governors and satraps (minor rulers), who reacted most favourably.

Ezra is informed of the people's sin

Soon after his arrival, Ezra was informed by the Jewish governors that a number of mixed marriages had taken place. He learned with horror that among those who had married heathen wives were even priests, Levites, and leading citizens. As a sign of mourning, Ezra rent his clothes, fasted all day, and then implored God to pardon His people's sin. While he prayed, a large crowd gathered around and were deeply moved by Ezra's grief. Shecaniah, one of their leaders, then spoke on behalf of the people. He publicly acknowledged their guilt, and proposed that they should enter into a solemn undertaking

176

with God to dismiss their foreign wives. Ezra made the leaders take an oath that they would act accordingly.

The people
repudiate mixed
marriages

This undertaking was ratified at a national assembly held in Jerusalem, which all Jews, throughout the land, were required to attend. Failure to do so would result in their expulsion from the community and the confiscation of their property. The people gathered in Jerusalem on the twentieth day of the ninth month (Kislev), in pouring rain. After Ezra had addressed them, they readily consented to his demands. As it would take some time to probe into each case of suspected intermarriage, it was decided to set up special commissions of lay and religious leaders in each city to examine individual offenders. After three months the commissions completed their task and submitted their report. This showed that, in all, seventeen priests, ten Levites, and eighty-six Israelites had contracted forbidden marriages, all of which were annulled.

Having completed his task, Ezra probably returned home. As soon as his back was turned, a number of people reverted to their former sinful practice, and again married heathen wives.

Readings from the Bible

Ezra, chapter 1, verses 1 to 4	Cyrus' proclamation
Ezra, chapter 4, verses 1 to 6	The Samaritans intervene
Haggai, chapter 1	Haggai's encouraging message
Ezra, chapter 7, verses 11 to 26	Decree of Artaxerxes
Ezra, chapter 10, verses 9 to 17	Ezra addresses the national assembly

Exercises

1. Give a brief account of the actions taken by (*a*) Cyrus, (*b*) Zerubbabel, (*c*) Haggai and Zechariah, (*d*) Darius, with regard to the building of the Temple.
2. Who were the Samaritans? Why did they interfere with the building of the Temple and city walls?
3. Give the main events in the story of Esther. When is this book read in the Synagogue, and why?
4. Write briefly on the following:
   (*a*) Cyrus' Cylinder; (*b*) the prophet Malachi; (*c*) Ezra's reforms.

26

NEHEMIAH

*The Jews are
threatened on
all sides*

ABOUT ten years had passed since Ezra had carried out his religious reforms. During this period the Jews of Judea were more concerned with physical security than with religious observance. Early in his reign, Artaxerxes had forbidden the restoration of the walls of Jerusalem (see page 175), and the Jews in the city were in the dangerous position of being unable to defend themselves against enemy attacks, which threatened from all sides. The Samaritans had long been troublesome and now the Edomites, Ammonites and Philistines, too, were waiting for the opportunity to take the offensive. The danger was averted by the timely intervention of Nehemiah, a loyal Jew, who was dedicated to his people's cause. He occupied the important position of royal cup-bearer at the Persian court, and enjoyed the king's confidence.

*Nehemiah goes to
his people's
assistance*

In the year 445 B.C.E., the twentieth year of Artaxerxes' reign, Nehemiah was told about conditions in Jerusalem by his kinsman, Hanani, who, with others, had come from Judea on a visit to Shushan. The grave news disturbed Nehemiah so much that he spent the next few days in deep mourning, and prayed earnestly to God for His aid in obtaining the king's permission to go and help his people. A suitable opportunity presented itself four months later, when Artaxerxes and his queen were dining. The king saw that his cup-bearer was unhappy, and on learning the cause, readily granted Nehemiah's request for leave of absence to go to Jerusalem, and empowered

178

him to rebuild the city's walls. The king not only reversed his previous order sent to Rehum (see page 175) but appointed Nehemiah governor of Judah, and provided him with an armed escort and letters of safe conduct. In addition, he was authorized to obtain the timber he needed from the royal forests in Judah.

Rapid progress is made in the rebuilding of Jerusalem's walls

Three days after his arrival in Jerusalem, Nehemiah, accompanied by a few trusted friends, secretly surveyed the ruined walls by night to assess the damage, and prepared his plans for their restoration. He then informed the Jewish leaders of his plans, which had the king's full support. They could not fail to be impressed and took immediate steps to organize a labour force. Workmen, recruited from every section of the entire community, were divided into groups, each being responsible for building or repairing a specific section of the walls. Even the High Priest, Eliashib, joined by his fellow priests, shared in the work by building the 'sheep gate', through which the animals entered the Temple grounds for sacrifice. Jericho was but one of several towns which supplied gangs of labourers. Members of the trade guilds of goldsmiths and merchants readily gave a hand. These, and many others, worked with such zeal and enthusiasm that they were soon well ahead of schedule.

The Samaritans renew their opposition

The Samaritans now renewed their opposition. Their leader at this time was Sanballat, the Horonite, governor of Samaria, who together with Tobiah, the Ammonite, and Geshem the Arabian, at first made fun of Nehemiah's efforts. But when they saw the work progressing so rapidly, they became seriously alarmed, and began to plot an attack against Jerusalem by bands of Arabians, Ammonites and Philistines. Nehemiah was faced with a serious problem. There was no point in appealing direct to Artaxerxes, for communications would take many months. Besides, there was always the danger that the king might become suspicious and re-impose his ban. To add to Nehemiah's troubles, his labourers complained of overwork, and the outlying towns were pleading for the return of their able-bodied men to protect them from attack. Nehemiah proved himself equal to the occasion. He armed all his workmen, and divided them into two groups so that while one was engaged in building, the other kept guard against attack. Nehemiah's trumpeter stayed constantly at his side, ready to give the alarm. Labourers who lived outside the city were ordered to remain in Jerusalem at night, to strengthen the defences. Within fifty-two days the task was completed, and it only remained for the city gates to be set up.

Sanballat's intrigues end in failure

Bitterly disappointed at their failure, Sanballat and his companions began to hatch new plots. They invited Nehemiah to meet them in a nearby village to talk over matters, with the obvious intention of assassinating him. Nehemiah replied that he could not really spare the time. Four times the invitation was repeated and refused, so finally the cunning Samaritans sent him a letter accusing him of a plot to proclaim himself king of Judah. Nehemiah contemptuously dismissed this as sheer imagination. They even went so far as to hire the false prophet Shemaiah to trap him, by suggesting that he take shelter in the Temple, as his life was in danger. Nehemiah quickly saw through this plot as an attempt to accuse him of cowardice and discredit him before the people.

All difficulties having been overcome, the massive gates were placed in position, and Nehemiah appointed his kinsman Hanani with Hananiah, the garrison commander, to govern Jerusalem. He instructed them to keep the gates closed at night and to open them well after dawn, to prevent any surprise attack before the citizens were up and about. Furthermore, a rota of householders was formed to keep watch at night.

Nehemiah faces internal problems

Amidst all this anxiety, Nehemiah had to face a number of problems affecting his own countrymen. The poorer section of the community, many of whom had left their normal occupations to build the walls, complained that they could not afford to feed their families. They had been forced to borrow money at a very high interest from their richer neighbours to buy food and pay the king's taxes. Some had been forced to mortgage their lands and vineyards and had even sold their families into slavery to pay their debts.

Nehemiah, in great anger, attacked the rich offenders for their heartless conduct and made them take a solemn oath to restore the property held on mortgage and to refund the excessive

180

interest they had charged. It is to Nehemiah's credit that during the twelve years of his administration, he set an example by cancelling taxes imposed on the people to pay his salary, even though he provided daily hospitality for a substantial number of Jewish resident officials and occasional guests.

Ezra reads and expounds the Law of Moses

Nehemiah now took the final step of re-establishing Jerusalem as the religious and spiritual centre of the Jewish people. Recalling Ezra from Persia, he summoned the entire nation to Jerusalem, where they gathered in the square before the water gate, on the first day of Tishri — the festival of the New Year. In response to the people's request, Ezra, standing on a wooden platform, read from the Law of Moses from early morning

Ezra reads the Law

until noon. At his side stood thirteen Levites who assisted Ezra by translating the Hebrew text, section by section, into Aramaic and adding their explanations so that the people could fully understand the meaning of the commandments.

The Torah readings produced a similar effect to that made on Josiah (see page 153). The people wept when they realized their disobedience to God's law but Nehemiah, supported by Ezra and the Levites, told them to refrain from sorrow on the holy day and to rejoice. On the following day, Ezra resumed his readings to a special gathering of priests, Levites, and lay leaders and reached the passage in the Book of Leviticus dealing with the observance of the Feast of Tabernacles on the fifteenth day of Tishri. In great excitement the people gathered branches of olive, myrtle and palm trees, made booths, and lived in them for seven days. The readings from the Law continued every day of the feast, and the eighth day was observed as a 'solemn assembly', in accordance with the law of the Torah.

The people pledge themselves to observe the commandments

On the twenty-fourth day of Tishri, a special fast was observed at which the people took an oath to be true to God's laws. A solemn covenant was drawn up, by which they bound themselves to observe the commandments, and this was signed, on their behalf, by Nehemiah and representative priests, Levites and lay leaders. They particularly pledged themselves not to marry their children to foreigners; not to trade on the Sabbath day; not to cultivate the soil during the Sabbatical year, and to forgive all debts incurred in the previous six years; to pay an annual tax of one third of a shekel to maintain the Temple service; and to provide for the priests and Levites by paying them their dues of first-fruits and tithes, respectively.

Quite a different decision was taken while the people were assembled in Jerusalem. The city had few permanent inhabitants and unless the population was substantially increased, its security would be endangered. It was therefore unanimously decided that one Jew out of every ten should be elected by lot to make his home in the capital. A number of volunteers also came forward, and received the nation's gratitude for their patriotism.

Before the people returned home, the city walls were dedicated in an atmosphere of joy. Two processions, led by Ezra and Nehemiah, set out in opposite directions, and went round the wall, meeting by the Temple. Their shouts of joy were heard far and wide over the hills of Judah.

Nehemiah pays a second visit to Jerusalem

In 433 B.C.E., Nehemiah returned to Persia, but, as was the case with Ezra, his absence from Judah encouraged his former enemies to re-assert themselves. This disquieting news led him to obtain Artaxerxes' permission to return to Jerusalem. He found that many Jews had broken their solemn promise and had married foreign wives. The High Priest, Eliashib, had set a bad example by permitting his grandson to marry Sanballat's daughter, and had even allowed Tobiah the Ammonite to occupy one of the Temple-rooms, formerly used as a storehouse for the Levites' provisions. Nehemiah immediately expelled Eliashib's grandson from the priesthood, turned Tobiah out of

182

the Temple, and ordered the room to be purified and restored to its proper use.

Nehemiah preserves the holiness of the Sabbath day

The Levites, he found, had been deprived of their tithes, and had left for their own cities, so that the Temple was deserted. Nehemiah brought them back, ordered the people to bring tithes, and appointed honest treasurers to supervise their collection and distribution. To his horror, Nehemiah witnessed the shameful desecration of the Sabbath throughout the country. Goods were brought into Jerusalem on the Sabbath, and the gates were crowded with Tyrian merchants who sold their fish and other goods to willing customers. Nehemiah had the city gates closed during the Sabbath and instructed the guards to see that his orders were obeyed. The merchants then set up their stalls outside, hoping that the people would leave Jerusalem on the Sabbath to buy their wares. They soon disappeared when Nehemiah threatened to arrest them. His final act was to force those Jews who had married foreign women to take an oath to send them away.

The achievements of Ezra and Nehemiah set the stage for a new era in Jewish history. Both these great leaders had established the teachings of the Torah as the supreme authority governing the lives of the Jewish people. Kingdoms were to arise and kingdoms pass away, but the written word, supplemented by oral tradition, was to prove the main source of Israel's miraculous preservation through the ages.

———————⇒•⇐———————

Readings from the Bible

Nehemiah, chapters 1 and 2 — Nehemiah comes to Jerusalem
Nehemiah, chapter 3, verses 1 to 32 — The city walls are rebuilt
Nehemiah, chapter 13, verses 10 to 30 — Nehemiah's reforms
Leviticus, chapter 25, verses 1 to 7
  and Deuteronomy, chapter 15,
  verses 1 to 6 — The Sabbatical year

Exercises

1. Show how Nehemiah dealt with the external and internal difficulties he had to face.
2. Describe Nehemiah's religious reforms.
3. Write briefly on the following:
   (*a*) Sanballat; (*b*) The Aramaic language; (*c*) the Sabbatical year; (*d*) Tobiah the Ammonite.

INDEX

Laban, 11
Lachish, siege of, 145
Leah, 11
Levites, 31 and freq.
Lot, 3ff

Machpelah, cave of, purchased by Abraham, 7
Mahanaim, Ishbosheth reigns there, 80; David retreats to, 89
Makkedah, cave of, 48
Malachi, the prophet, 175
Manasseh, king of Judah, 151
Manna, 25, 46
Megiddo, Josiah killed there, 155
Melchizedek, priest of Jerusalem, 4
Menahem, king of Israel, 138
Merodach-baladan, king of Babylon, 144
Mesha, king of Moab, 119
Micah, the prophet, 149
Michal, David's wife, 72
Michmas, battle of, 68
Midianites, 56
Miriam, sister of Moses, 34, 37
Mizpah, Saul chosen king there, 67
Moabite stone, 119
Moabites, 39, 119
Moses, call of, 22; before Pharaoh, 23; at Mt. Sinai, 28; commanded to erect Sanctuary, 30; consecrates priests, 31; strikes rock, 37; appoints Joshua as his successor, 41; death of, 43

Naaman, cured of leprosy, 122
Nabal, his churlishness to David, 75
Naboth, the murder of, 112
Nadab, king of Israel, 104
Nathan, the prophet, confirms kingdom to David, 83; denounces David's sin, 86
Nebo, Mt., 43
Nebuchadnezzar, captures Jerusalem, 161
Nebuzaradan, 161
Nehemiah, 178ff; rebuilds Jerusalem, 179; Sanballat's opposition, 179; religious reforms, 182

Nob, David at, 74; Saul massacres the priests, 74

Obadiah, overseer of Ahab's house, 107
Obed-edom, 83
Omri, usurps the throne of Israel, 106; builds Samaria, 107

Paran, wilderness of, 35
Pashhur, 157
Passover, celebration of, 24, 46, 143, 154, 174
Pekah, king of Israel, defeated by the Assyrians, 140
Pekahiah, king of Israel, 139
Persian empire, 171ff
Pharaoh, king of Egypt, 20ff
Pharaoh-hophra, 160
Pharaoh-necho, defeats Josiah, 155; takes Jehoiahaz captive, 157; defeated by Nebuchadnezzar, 158
Philistines, Samson's exploits against them, 59ff; capture the ark, 64; defeated at Mizpah and Michmas, 65, 68; their invasion under Achish, 78; their victory at Gilboa, 79; David's conquest over them, 83
Plagues, the ten, 23
Potiphar, 15
Pul, king of Assyria, attacks Israel, 138

Rabbah, besieged by Joab, 85
Rab-shakeh, the, 146
Rachel, 11ff
Rahab, protects the spies, 45
Ramah, the residence of Samuel, 65
Ramoth-gilead, battle of, 114
Rebekah, 8ff
Red Sea, crossing of, 25
Rehoboam, king of Judah, 101
Rehum, 175
Rephidim, 26
Revolt of the ten tribes, 101
Rezin, king of Syria, 139
Ruth, story of, 61
Samaria, 107
Samaritans, 173ff
Samson, 59ff

188

Samuel, his call, 63; becomes judge, 65; anoints Saul as king, 66; rebukes Saul at Gilgal, 68; anoints David, 70; his death, 75

Sanballat, his opposition to Nehemiah, 179f

Sarah, 3ff

Sargon II, king of Assyria, captures Samaria, 141

Saul, anointed by Samuel, 66; elected king, 67; defeats the Ammonites, 67; rebuked by Samuel, 68; his jealousy of David, 72; his cruelty at Nob, 74; spared by David, 75, 76; his death, 78

Sennacherib invades Judah, 145

Shallum, king of Israel, 138

Shalmaneser, king of Assyria invades Israel, 141

Shaphan, the scribe, 158

Sheba, queen of, visits Solomon, 98

Shechem, Abraham builds his first altar, 3; Jacob lives there, 12; Joseph buried, 48; Joshua assembles the tribes, 52; Rehoboam crowned as king, 101

Shemaiah, the prophet, 102

Shiloh, 64

Shishak, king of Egypt, despoils the temple, 102

Sinai, Mt., 28

Sisera, 55

Sodom and Gomorrah, 5

Solomon, 93ff; his wisdom, 94; builds the Temple, 95; trade relations, 98; his decline and death, 99

Spies, the twelve sent by Moses, 35; the two sent by Joshua, 45

Sumerians, 1f

Syrians, 111ff

Tabernacle, the, 30

Tabernacles, feast of, 96, 103, 172, 181

Tabor, Mt., 56

Tattenai, Persian governor, 173

Temple, site purchased by David, 91; building by Solomon, 95; despoiled by Shishak, 102; repaired by Joash, 130; despoiled by Nebuchadnezzar, 161; its destruction, 161; its rebuilding, 173

Ten commandments, 28

Terah, 2

Tiglath-pileser, king of Assyria, 138

Two and a half tribes, 42

Ur, city of, 2

Uriah the Hittite, 85

Uzziah, king of Judah, 134

Xerxes, king of Persia, 174

Zadok, the priest, anoints Solomon, 91

Zechariah, king of Israel, 136

Zechariah, the prophet, 173

Zedekiah, king of Judah, 160; taken captive to Babylon, 161

Zerubbabel, 172

Zimri, 106